THE ULTIMATE
Low Fat Baking
COOKBOOK

THE ULTIMATE
Low Fat Baking
COOKBOOK

The best-ever step-by-step collection of low-fat baking recipes for
tempting and healthy eating

Consulting Editor: Linda Fraser

HERMES
HOUSE

This edition first published in 1998 by Hermes House
27 West 20th Street, New York, NY 10011

HERMES HOUSE books are available for bulk
purchase for sales promotion and for premium use.
For details, write or call the sales director,
Hermes House, 27 West 20th Street, New York,
NY 10011; (800) 354-9657.

© Anness Publishing Limited 1998

Hermes House is an imprint of
Anness Publishing Limited

ISBN 1 84038 061 6

Publisher: Joanna Lorenz
Senior Editor: Cathy Marriott
Designer: Lilian Lindblom
Illustrations: Anna Koska

Printed and bound in China

10 9 8 7 6 5 4 3 2

Contents

Introduction

When we talk of cakes and baking we tend to imagine rich, calorie-laden treats that are well out of reach if you are following a low-fat diet. With reduced-fat cooking methods, however, it is very easy to create delicious, low-fat desserts, cakes and other baked goods that are also full of flavor and appeal. It is generally agreed that a high-fat diet is bad for us, especially if the fats are of the saturated variety. And unless you are making meringues or angel food cakes, it is rarely possible to do entirely without fat in baking. Nevertheless, it is possible to cut down considerably on the amount used, and equally good results can be achieved using unsaturated oils instead of saturated fats.

Polyunsaturated oils such as sunflower oil, corn oil and safflower oil are excellent for most baking purposes, but choose olive oil, which is monounsaturated, for recipes that require a good, strong flavor. When an oil is not suitable, a soft margarine that is high in polyunsaturates is the fat to choose. Low-fat spreads are ideal for spreading but not good for baking, because they contain a high proportion of water.

Although cheese is high in saturated fat, its flavor makes it invaluable in many recipes. Choose reduced-fat varieties with a sharp flavor, or a smaller amount of a highly flavored cheese such as Parmesan. When using less fat, you can add extra moisture to cakes and tea breads in the form of fresh or dried fruits. There is no need to use whole milk—try skim milk or fruit juice instead. Buttermilk is, surprisingly, low in fat and is perfect for soda bread and scones. Cream undoubtedly adds a touch of luxury to special-occasion cakes; however, fromage frais, thick yogurt or ricotta cheese sweetened with honey make delicious low-fat fillings and toppings for even the most elaborate cakes.

So you will see that using less fat doesn't prevent you from making scrumptious cakes, cookies, biscuits and bars that look and taste every bit as good as those made traditionally with butter and cream. The recipes in this book are sure to inspire, impress and amaze everyone who believed low-fat baking to be an idea too good to be true.

Left: Everyone loves fresh breads, scones and cookies straight from the oven.

Pantry

Cutting down on fat doesn't mean sacrificing taste. Instead, choose ingredients that are naturally lower in fat. This is not as limiting as it sounds, as the following ingredients show.

FLOURS

Mass-produced, highly refined flours are fine for most baking purposes, but for the very best results choose organic stone-ground flours, because they will add flavor as well as texture to your baking.

Rye flour

This dark-colored flour has a low gluten content and gives a dense loaf with a good flavor. It is best mixed with wheat flour to give a lighter loaf.

Cake flour

This flour contains less gluten than all-purpose flour and is ideal for light cakes and biscuits.

Bread flour

Made from hard wheat, which contains a high proportion of gluten, this flour is the one to use for bread making.

Whole-wheat flour

Because this flour contains the complete wheat kernel, it gives a coarser texture and a good, wholesome flavor to bread.

NUTS AND SEEDS

Most nuts are low in saturated fats and high in polyunsaturated fats. Use them sparingly as their total fat content is high. Sunflower seeds and poppy seeds are good for decorating rolls or adding texture.

YEAST

Yeast causes bread to rise.

HERBS AND SPICES

Chopped fresh herbs add a great deal of interest to baking. They add flavor to breads, scones and soda breads. In the absence of fresh herbs, dried herbs can be used: Less is needed but the flavor is generally not as good.

Spices can add either strong or subtle flavors, depending on the amount used. Ground cinnamon, nutmeg and apple pie spice are most useful for baking, but more exotic spices, such as saffron or cardamom, can also be used to great effect.

Buy herbs and spices from a store with a high turnover to ensure optimum freshness and flavor.

SWEETENERS

Dried fruits

These are a traditional addition to cakes and tea breads. There is a wide range available, including unusual varieties such as peach, pineapple, banana and mango, as well as the more familiar currants and candied cherries. Natural sugars in dried fruits add sweetness to baked goods and keep them moist, making it possible to use less fat.

Fruit juice

Concentrated fruit juices are very useful for baking. They have no added sweeteners or preservatives and can be diluted as required. Use them in their concentrated form for baking or for sweetening fillings.

Honey

Good honey has a strong flavor, so you can use less of it than the equivalent amount of sugar. It also contains traces of minerals and vitamins.

Malt extract

This is a sugary by-product of barley, available in health food stores. It has a strong flavor and is ideal for bread, cakes and tea breads, as it adds moisture.

Molasses

This is the residue left after the first stage of refining sugar cane. It has a strong, smoky and slightly bitter taste that gives a good flavor to baked goods.

Pear and apple or other fruit spread

This is a very concentrated fruit juice with no added sugar. It has a sweet-sour taste and can be used as a spread or blended with a little fruit juice and added to baking recipes as a sweetener.

Unrefined sugars

Most baking recipes call for sugar; choose unrefined sugar rather than refined sugars, as they have more flavor and contain some minerals.

Right: It's easier to follow a healthy eating plan if you have a pantry full of tempting ingredients that are naturally low in fat.

flour

canned apricots

dried pineapple

dry yeast

light brown sugar

currants   poppy seeds   honey   herbs

it   oatmeal   cinnamon sticks   dried apricots   sesame seeds

sunflower seeds

gooseberries

flax seed

ns   candied cherries   olive oil   pear and apple spread   apricot compote   dates

extra virgin olive oil

fresh fruit

rolled oats

orange juice

blueberries

Oils, Fats and Dairy Products

OIL AND FAT ALTERNATIVES

Low-fat spreads are ideal for spreading on breads and tea breads, but are unfortunately not suitable for baking because they have a high water content.

When you are baking, try to avoid saturated fats such as butter and hard margarine and use oils high in polyunsaturates such as sunflower, corn or safflower oil. When margarine is essential, choose a variety that is high in polyunsaturates.

Low-fat spread, rich buttermilk blend

Made with a high proportion of buttermilk, which is naturally low in fat. Unsuitable for baking.

Olive oil

Use this monounsaturated oil when a recipe requires a good strong flavor. It is best to use extra virgin olive oil.

Olive oil reduced-fat spread

Based on olive oil, this spread has a better flavor that some other low-fat spreads, but is not suitable for baking.

Reduced-fat butter

This contains about 40% fat; the rest is water and milk solids emulsified together. It is not suitable for baking.

Sunflower light

Not suitable for baking, as it contains only 40% fat, plus emulsified water and milk solids.

Sunflower oil

High in polyunsaturates, this is the oil used most frequently in this book, as it has a pleasant but not too dominant flavor.

Very low fat spread

Contains only 20–30% fat and so is not suitable for baking.

LOW-FAT CHEESES

There are a lot of low-fat cheeses that can be used in baking. Generally, harder cheeses have a higher fat content than soft cheeses. Choose aged cheese whenever possible, as you need less of it to give a good flavor.

Cottage cheese

A low-fat soft cheese that is also available in a reduced-fat form.

Ricotta cheese

This is a low-fat soft cheese made with either skim or low-fat milk and can be used instead of cream cheese.

Edam and Maasdam

Two medium-fat hard cheeses well suited to baking.

Feta

This is a medium-fat cheese with a firm, crumbly texture. It has a slightly sour, salty flavor that can range from rather bland to strong.

Reduced-fat Cheddar and Red Leicester

These contain about 14% fat.

Mozzarella light

This is a reduced-fat version of an Italian soft cheese.

Quark

Made from fermented skim milk, this soft, white cheese is virtually free of fat.

CREAM ALTERNATIVES

Yogurt and fromage frais make excellent alternatives to cream, and when combined with honey, liqueurs or other flavorings they make delicious fillings or toppings for cakes and other baked goods.

Yogurt

This contains friendly bacterial cultures that aid digestion. Yogurt has a mild, sweet taste.

Crème fraîche

This thick sour cream has a mild, lemony taste. Look for reduced-fat crème fraîche, which has a fat content of 15%.

Fromage frais

This is a fresh soft cheese available in two grades: virtually fat free (0.4% fat) and a more creamy variety (7.9% fat).

Strained plain yogurt

This thick, creamy yogurt is made from whole milk with a fat content of 10%. A low-fat version is also available.

olive oil

sunflower oil

buttermilk blend

sunflower oil

very low fat spread

olive oil reduced-fat spread

reduced-fat butter

Left: Try to avoid using saturated fats, such as butter and margarine. Instead use oils or spreads high in polyunsaturates.

ricotta cheese

cottage cheese

mozzarella

Edam

Maasdam

Cheddar

feta

Red Leicester

soft cheese

quark

low-fat milk

buttermilk

low-fat yogurt

reduced-fat crème fraîche

eggs

yogurt

light fromage frais

Above: There is a whole range of low-fat cheeses that can be used in baking.

Left: Use low-fat milk for baking and try yogurt or fromage frais as an alternative to cream.

LOW-FAT MILKS

Buttermilk
Made from skim milk with a bacterial culture added, it is very low in fat.

Non-fat dry milk
A useful low-fat standby.

Low-fat milk
With a fat content of only 1 or 2%, this milk tastes less rich than whole milk. It is favored by many people for everyday use for precisely this reason.

Skim milk
This milk has had virtually all fat removed, leaving 0.1–0.3%. It is ideal for those wishing to cut down their fat intake.

EGGS
These are essential for baking.

Equipment

If you choose good-quality, heavy nonstick cookware, the amount of fat used in baking can be kept to an absolute minimum.

Baking parchment

For lining pans and baking sheets to ensure that cakes do not stick.

Baking sheet

Choose a large, heavy baking sheet that will not warp at high temperatures.

Balloon whisk

Perfect for whisking egg whites and incorporating air into other light mixtures.

Box grater

This multipurpose grater can be used for citrus rind, fruit and vegetables, and cheese.

Brown paper

Used for wrapping around the outside of cake pans to protect the cake batter from the full heat of the oven.

Cake tester

A simple implement that, when inserted into a cooked cake, will come out clean if the cake is ready.

Chef's knife

This has a heavy, wide blade and is ideal for chopping.

Deep round cake pan

This deep pan is ideal for baking fruit cakes.

Electric mixer

Ideal for creaming cake mixtures, whipping cream and whisking egg whites.

Honey dipper

For spooning honey without making a mess.

Icing spatula

This implement is needed for loosening pies, tarts and breads from baking sheets and for smoothing icing over cakes.

Jelly roll pan

This shallow pan is designed especially for jelly rolls.

Juicer

Made from porcelain, glass or plastic—used for squeezing the juice from citrus fruits.

Layer cake pan

Ideal for sponge cakes; make sure you have two of them!

Loaf pan

Available in various sizes and used for making loaf-shaped breads and tea breads.

Measuring jug

Absolutely essential for measuring any kind of liquid accurately.

Measuring spoons

Standard measuring spoons are essential for measuring small quantities of ingredients.

Mixing bowls

A set of different-size bowls is essential in any kitchen for whisking and mixing.

Muffin pan

Shaped into individual cups, this pan is much simpler to use than individual paper liners. It can also be used for baking small pies and tarts.

Nutmeg grater

This miniature grater is used for grating whole nutmeg.

Nylon sieve

Suitable for most baking purposes, and particularly for sieving foods that react adversely with metal.

Paring knife

A knife for preparing the fruit and vegetables that you add to your baked goods.

Pastry brush

Useful for brushing excess flour from pastry and brushing glazes over pastries and breads.

Pastry cutters

A variety of shapes and sizes of cutter are useful when stamping out pastry, biscuits, cookies and scones.

Rectangular cake pan

For making sheet cakes, brownies and bars, served cut into slices.

Ring mold

Perfect for making angel food cakes and other ring-shaped cakes.

Scissors

Vital for cutting paper and snipping dough and pastry.

Square cake pan

Used for making square cakes or cakes served cut into smaller squares.

Wire rack

Ideal for cooling cakes and other baked goods, allowing the circulation of air, which will prevent sogginess.

Wire sieve

A large wire sieve is ideal for most normal baking purposes.

Wooden spoon

Essential for mixing ingredients and creaming mixtures.

Right: Invest in a few useful items for easy low-fat cooking: Nonstick cookware and accurate measuring equipment are essential.

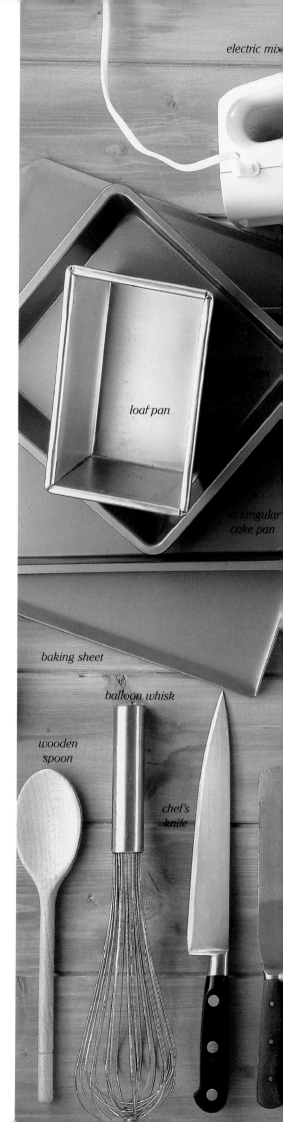

electric mixer

loaf pan

rectangular cake pan

baking sheet

balloon whisk

wooden spoon

chef's knife

baking parchment

mixing bowls

brown paper

scissors

layer cake pan

ring mold

pastry brush

wire rack

measuring jug

pastry
cutters

deep round
cake pan

paring knife

honey
dipper

wire rack

jelly roll pan

juicer

nutmeg
grater

box grater

wire sieve

nylon sieve

measuring
spoons

muffin pan

Facts about Fat

It's easy to cut down on obvious sources of fat, such as butter, margarine, cream, whole milk and high-fat cheeses, but watch out for "hidden" fats.

Most of us eat more fat every day than the 10g that our bodies need; on average we each consume about 115g fat each day. Current nutritional advice isn't quite that strict on fat intake, though, and it suggests that we should limit our daily intake to no more than 30% of total calories. In real terms, this means that for an average intake of 2,000 calories a day, 30% of energy would come from about 600 calories. Since each gram of fat provides 9 calories, your total daily intake should be no more than 67g fat.

Although we may think of cakes and cookies as sweet foods, more calories come from their fat than from their sugar. Indeed, of the quarter of our fat intake that comes from nonmeat sources, a fifth comes from dairy products and margarine and the rest from cakes, cookies, pastries and other foods. The merits of low-fat baking are enormous, as you are able not only to cut down on your fat intake in general, but you also have control over exactly how

much fat you and your family consume on a daily basis and the type of fat it is.

Fats can be divided into two main categories—saturated and unsaturated. We are all well aware of the dangers of saturated fats in relation to blocking arteries and causing coronary heart disease. Much of the saturated fat we eat comes from animal sources—meat and dairy products such as suet, lard and butter—which are solid at room temperature. However, there are also some saturated fats of vegetable origin, notably coconut and palm oils. In addition, a number of margarines are "hydrogenated," a process that increases the proportion of saturated fat they contain. Such margarine should be avoided.

Above: Animal products such as butter, lard, suet and some margarines are major sources of saturated fats.

Left: Some oils, such as olive oil and canola, are thought to help lower blood cholesterol.

The Fat and Calorie Contents of Food

This chart shows the weight of fat and the energy content of 110g (3½ ounces) of various foods.

Unsaturated fats can be divided into two main types: monounsaturated and poly-unsaturated. Monounsaturated fats are found in various foods including olive oil, canola oil and some nuts. These fats may actually lower blood cholesterol, and this could explain why in Mediterranean countries, where olive oil is widely consumed, there is such a low incidence of heart disease.

The most familiar polyunsaturated fats are of vegetable or plant origin and include sunflower oil, corn oil, soybean oil, walnut oil and many soft margarines. It was believed at one time that it was beneficial to switch to polyunsaturated fats, as they may also help lower cholesterol. Today, however, most experts believe that it is more important to reduce the total intake of all kinds of fat.

Above: Vegetable oils and some margarines are high in polyunsaturated fat.

FRUIT AND NUTS	Fat	Calories
Apples, eating	0.1g	47
Avocados	19.5g	190
Bananas	0.3g	95
Dried mixed fruit	1.6g	227
Grapefruit	0.1g	30
Oranges	0.1g	37
Peaches	0.1g	33
Almonds	55.8g	612
Brazil nuts	68.2g	682
Peanut butter, smooth	53.7g	623
Pine nuts	68.6g	688

DAIRY PRODUCE, FATS AND OILS	Fat	Calories
Cream, heavy	48.0g	449
Cream, light	19.1g	198
Cream, whipping	39.3g	373
Milk, skim	0.1g	33
Milk, whole	3.9g	66
Cheddar cheese	34.4g	412
Cheddar type, reduced fat	15.0g	216
Cream cheese	47.4g	439
Brie	26.9g	319
Edam	25.4g	333
Feta	20.2g	250
Parmesan	32.7g	452
Strained plain yogurt	9.1g	115
Low-fat yogurt, plain	0.8g	56
Butter	81.7g	737
Lard	99.0g	891
Low-fat spread	40.5g	390
Margarine	81.6g	739
Coconut oil	99.9g	899
Corn oil	99.9g	899
Olive oil	99.9g	899
Safflower oil	99.9g	899
Eggs (whole)	10.9g	147
Egg white	trace	36
Egg yolk	30.5g	339

OTHER FOODS	Fat	Calories
Sugar	0	94
Chocolate, milk	30.3g	529
Honey	0	88
Jam	0	61
Marmalade	0	61
Lemon curd	5.1g	283

Techniques

Baking is easy and satisfying, even if you're a beginner. Just follow the recipes, the tips and the step-by-step techniques and you will get perfect results every time.

1 For liquids measured in jugs: Use a glass or clear plastic measuring jug. Put the jug on a flat surface and pour in the liquid. Bend down and check that the liquid is exactly level with the marking on the jug as specified in the recipe.

2 For measuring dry ingredients in a spoon: Fill the spoon with the ingredient. Level the surface even with the brim of the spoon, using the straight edge of a knife.

3 For liquids measured in spoons: Pour the liquid into the measuring spoon to the brim, and then pour it into the mixing bowl.

4 For measuring flour in a cup or spoon: Scoop the flour from the canister or bag in the measuring cup or spoon. Hold it over the canister or bag and level the surface.

5 For measuring butter: Cut off the specified amount following the markings on the wrapping paper.

6 For rectangular and square cake pans: Fold the paper and crease it with your fingernail to fit snugly into the corners of the pan. Then press the bottom paper lining into place.

7 To line muffin pans: Use paper liners of the required size or grease and flour the pans.

Using Yeast

There are three main types of yeast currently available—active dry, rapid-rise and fresh. Rapid-rise is added directly to the dry ingredients, whereas dry and fresh yeast must first be mixed with warm liquid and a little sugar to activate them.

USING ACTIVE DRY YEAST

1 Measure dry yeast, then sprinkle it into the warm liquid in a jug or small bowl with a pinch of sugar. Stir well and set aside in a warm place for about 10–15 minutes.

2 When the yeast liquid becomes frothy, stir into the dry ingredients.

Cook's Tip
Active dry yeast doesn't dissolve well in milk. You must either leave it for about 30 minutes to froth, or if you are in a hurry, dissolve it in a little water first.

USING RAPID-RISE YEAST

1 Add rapid-rise yeast to the dry ingredients directly from the package. Do not dissolve it in liquid first.

USING FRESH YEAST

1 Place fresh yeast in a small bowl with a pinch of sugar and a little lukewarm water. Cream together until smooth, then leave for 5–10 minutes until frothy, before adding to the dry ingredients.

Making Muffins and Quick Breads

As their name denotes, these are fast and easy to make. The rising agent reacts quickly with moisture and heat to make the muffins and breads rise, without the need for a rising period before baking.

The rising agent is usually baking soda or baking powder, which is a mixture of baking soda and an acid salt such as cream of tartar. It will start to work as soon as it comes into contact with liquid, so don't mix the dry and liquid ingredients until just before you are ready to fill the muffin pans and bake them.

In addition to the thick-batter quick breads discussed here, there are also quick breads such as scones that are made from soft doughs.

Cook's Tip

Rapid-rise (or easy-blend) yeast is available in the U.S., but is more commonly used in Europe. Unlike active dry yeast, there is no need to mix it with liquid. Just combine it with the flour and other dry ingredients and then add the warm liquids.

MUFFINS

1 Combine the dry ingredients in a bowl. It is a good idea to sift the flour with the rising agent, salt and any spices to mix them evenly. Add the liquid ingredients and stir just until the dry ingredients are moistened; the mixture will not be smooth. Do not overmix attempting to remove all the lumps. If you do, the muffins will be tough and will have air holes in them.

2 Divide the mixture evenly among the greased muffin-pan cups or paper liners, filling them about two-thirds full. Bake until golden brown and a wooden skewer inserted in the center comes out clean. To prevent soggy bottoms, remove the muffins immediately from the pans to a wire rack. Cool, and serve warm or at room temperature.

FRUIT AND NUT TEA BREADS

1 **Method 1**: Stir together all the liquid ingredients. Add the dry ingredients and beat just until smoothly blended. **Method 2**: Beat the butter with the sugar until the mixture is light and fluffy. Beat in the eggs followed by the other liquid ingredients. Stir in the dry ingredients. Pour the mixture into a prepared pan (typically a loaf pan). Bake until a wooden skewer inserted in the center comes out clean. If the bread is browning too quickly, cover the top with foil.

2 Cool in the pan for 5 minutes, then turn out onto a wire rack to cool completely. A lengthwise crack on the surface is characteristic of tea breads. For easier slicing, wrap the bread in waxed paper and wrap again in foil, then store overnight at room temperature.

Making Breadsticks and Focaccia

Italian flatbreads such as focaccia and breadsticks can be topped with herbs and seeds for tasty accompaniments or appetizers.

Personalize breadsticks and focaccia with combinations of your favorite ingredients for unusual snacks, or split and fill flatbreads with ham or cheese for an Italian-style sandwich. This basic dough can be used for other recipes, such as pizza. The uncooked dough may be frozen, and thawed before baking.

BREADSTICKS

1 There's no need for the first rising. Divide the dough into walnut-size pieces and roll out on a floured surface with your hands, into thin sausage shapes. Transfer to a greased baking sheet, cover and let sit in a warm place for 10–15 minutes. Bake until crisp.

FOCACCIA

1 Warm a mixing bowl by swirling some hot water in it. Drain. Place the yeast in the bowl and pour on the warm water. Stir in the sugar, mix with a fork, and allow to stand for 5–10 minutes, until the yeast has dissolved and starts to foam.

2 Use a wooden spoon to mix in the salt and about one-third of the flour. Mix in another third of the flour, stirring with the spoon until the dough forms a mass and begins to pull away from the sides of the bowl.

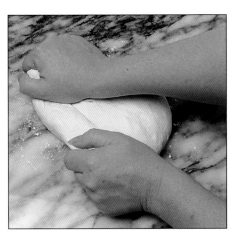

3 Sprinkle some of the remaining flour onto the smooth work surface. Remove the dough from the bowl and begin to knead it, working in the remaining flour a little at a time. Knead for 8–10 minutes. By the end the dough should be elastic and smooth. Form it into a ball.

4 Lightly oil a mixing bowl. Place the dough in the bowl. Stretch a damp dish towel or plastic wrap across the top of the bowl, and let stand in a warm place until the dough has doubled in volume, 40–50 minutes or more, depending on the type of yeast used. To test whether the dough has risen enough, poke two fingers into the dough. If the indentations remain, the dough is ready to use.

5 Punch the dough down with your fist to release the air. Knead for 1–2 minutes.

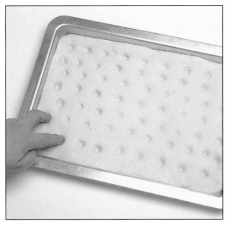

6 Brush a pan with oil. Press the dough into the pan with your fingers to a layer 1 inch thick. Cover and let rise for 30 minutes. Preheat the oven. Make indentations all over the focaccia with your fingers. Brush with oil, and bake until pale golden brown.

Making Scones and Popovers

Scones are quick breads made with a soft dough based on flour and milk, with a rising agent added.
Popovers are individual batter muffins, made in a similar way to Yorkshire puddings.

The dough of scones may be rolled out and cut into shapes, dropped from a spoon onto a baking sheet, or lightly patted out and then stamped out with a cutter into rounds or other shapes.

SCONES

1 Sift together the dry ingredients into a large mixing bowl (flour, baking powder with or without baking soda, salt, sugar, spices, etc.).

2 Add the fat (butter, margarine or vegetable fat). With a pastry blender or two knives, cut the fat into the dry ingredients until the mixture resembles fine crumbs, or rub in the fat with your fingertips.

3 Add the liquid ingredients (milk, cream, buttermilk, eggs). Stir with a fork until the dry ingredients are thoroughly moistened and will come together in a ball of fairly soft dough in the center of the bowl.

4 Turn the dough onto a lightly floured surface. Knead it very lightly, folding and pressing to mix evenly, for about 30 seconds. Roll or pat out the dough to 1 inch thick.

5 With a floured, sharp-edged cutter, cut out rounds or other shapes. Arrange on an ungreased baking sheet. Brush with beaten egg or cream. Bake until golden brown. Serve immediately.

6 For griddle scones: If using a well-seasoned cast-iron griddle, there is no need to grease it. Heat it slowly and evenly. Put scone triangles or rounds on the hot griddle and cook for 5–6 minutes on each side, or until golden brown and cooked through.

POPOVERS

1 Sift the flour into a large bowl along with other dry ingredients such as salt and ground black pepper. Make a well in the center of the dry ingredients and put in the eggs, egg yolks and some of the liquid.

2 With a wooden spoon, beat together the eggs and liquid in the well just to mix them. Gradually draw in some of the flour from the sides, stirring vigorously.

3 When the mixture is smooth, stir in the remaining liquid. Stir just until the ingredients are combined—the trick is not to overmix.

4 Pour the mixture into greased muffin pans or ramekins and bake until golden brown. Do not open the oven door during baking time or the popovers may collapse. Run a knife around the edge of each popover to loosen it, then turn out and serve hot.

Cutting Tips for Scones

Be sure the cutter or knife is sharp, so that the edges of the scone shapes are not compressed; this would prevent rising. Cut the shapes close together so that you won't have to re-roll the dough more than once. If necessary, a short, sturdy drinking glass can be pressed into service as a cutter. Flour the rim well and do not press too hard. When cutting out, don't twist the cutter.

Shaping Rolls

Bread rolls can be made in all sorts of interesting shapes and sizes. Begin by dividing the dough into even-size portions. Try these traditional variations first and then, when you are used to working with dough, experiment with your own designs.

1 To shape cottage rolls, divide each portion of dough into two pieces, making one piece about twice the size of the other. Shape both pieces into smooth balls. Dampen the top of the large ball and place the small ball on top. Push a lightly floured index finger through the middle of the dough.

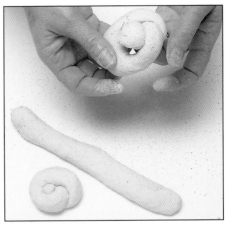

3 To shape knots, roll each dough portion into a fairly long sausage shape. Carefully knot the dough sausage, as you would a piece of string.

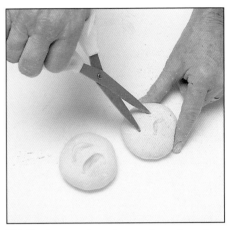

5 To shape snipped-top rolls, roll each dough portion into a smooth ball. Using a pair of kitchen scissors, make two or three snips in the top of each ball.

2 To shape cloverleaf rolls, divide each portion of dough into three equal-size pieces. Form each piece into a smooth ball, lightly dampen, and arrange in a cloverleaf formation. Press together lightly.

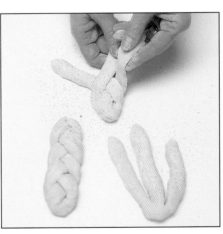

4 To shape braids, divide each dough portion into three equal pieces. Roll each piece into an even sausage shape. Dampen the three sausages at one end and pinch together. Braid the sausages loosely and pinch together at the other end, dampening lightly first.

6 To shape twists, divide each dough portion into two equal pieces. Roll each piece into an even sausage shape, then twist the two pieces together, dampening at each end and pressing together firmly.

Lining Baking Pans

Make sure that your cakes and tea breads don't stick by lining the pan with waxed paper or baking parchment. Use low-fat margarine or oil to lightly grease the pan if necessary.

LINING A ROUND PAN

1 To line a round pan, place the pan on waxed paper or baking parchment and draw around the edge. Cut out two circles that size, then cut a strip a little longer than the pan's circumference and one and a half times its depth. Lightly grease the pan and place one paper circle on the base. Make small diagonal cuts along one edge of the paper strip.

2 Put the paper strip inside the pan, with the snipped fringe along the bottom. Place the second paper circle in the bottom of the pan, covering the fringe. Grease once more.

LINING A JELLY ROLL PAN

1 To line a jelly roll pan, cut a piece of baking parchment or waxed paper large enough to line the bottom and sides of the pan. Lay the paper over the pan and make four diagonal cuts, one from each corner of the paper to the nearest corner of the pan.

2 Lightly grease the pan. Place the paper in the pan and smooth into the sides, overlapping the paper corners to fit neatly.

LINING A LOAF PAN

1 To line a loaf pan, cut a strip of waxed paper or baking parchment three times as long as the depth of the pan and as wide as the length of the bottom.

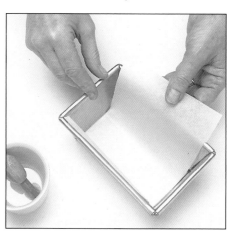

2 Lightly grease the pan. Place the strip of paper in the pan so that the paper covers the bottom and comes up over both long sides.

Testing Cakes

It is very important to check that cakes and other baked goods are properly cooked; otherwise they can be soggy, and cakes may sink in the middle.

TESTING A FRUIT CAKE

1 To test if a fruit cake is ready, push a skewer or cake tester into it; the cake is done if the skewer or cake tester comes out clean.

2 Fruit cakes are generally left to cool in the pan for 30 minutes. Then turn the cake out carefully, peel away the paper and place on a wire rack to cool completely.

TESTING A SPONGE CAKE

1 To test if a sponge cake is ready, press down lightly in the center of the cake with your fingertips—if the cake springs back, it is done.

2 To remove the baked sponge cake from the pan, loosen around the edge by carefully scraping around the inside of the pan with a metal spatula, invert the cake onto a wire rack, cover with a second rack, then invert again. Remove the top rack and allow to cool.

TESTING BREAD

1 To test if a loaf of bread is ready, first loosen the edges of the loaf with a metal spatula, then tip out the loaf.

2 Hold the loaf upside down and tap it gently on the bottom. If it sounds hollow, the bread is done.

Icing a Cake

Confident icing of a cake makes all the difference to its appearance. With just a little practice, your cakes will look completely professional!

MAKING A PASTRY BAG

Being able to make your own pastry bag is a very handy skill, particularly if you are dealing with small amounts of icing or several colors.

1 Fold a 10-inch square of baking parchment or waxed paper in half to form a triangle. Using the center of the long side as the central tip, roll half the paper into a cone.

2 Holding the paper in position, continue to roll the other half of the triangle around the first, to form a complete cone.

3 Holding the cone firmly, fold the end of the paper triangle over the top into the inside of the cone to secure it. Fill the bag no more than half full with icing, fold over the top several times to seal, then snip off the tip to the required size.

ICING A CAKE

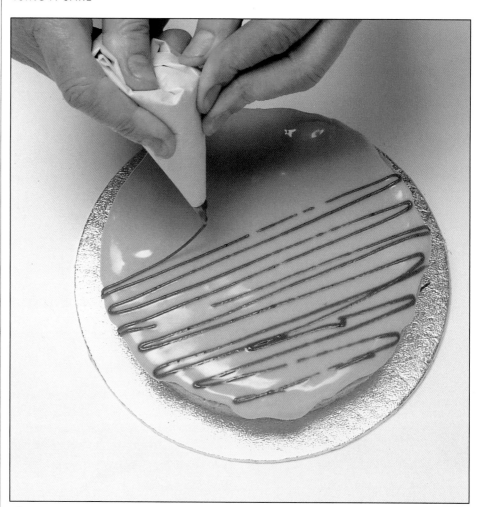

1 To create a simple zigzag effect, ice the cake all over, then pipe lines in a different color backward and forward over the top.

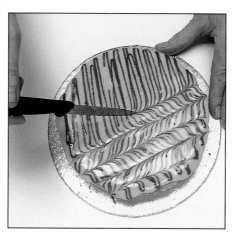

2 To create a feathered effect, follow step 1, then drag a knife through the icing at regular intervals in opposite directions, perpendicular to the lines.

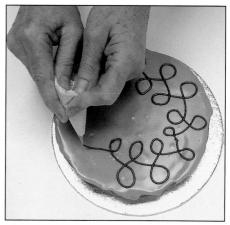

3 To make a figure eight, or a similar effect, ice the cake all over, then, using a different colored icing, pipe figure eights around the edge of the cake in a steady stream.

Preparing Glazes and Citrus Fruits

Apricot glaze is extremely useful for brushing over any kind of fresh fruit topping or filling to give it a lovely shiny appearance. Oranges, lemons and other citrus fruits are widely used in baking, both as flavoring and as decoration.

MAKING APRICOT GLAZE

PREPARING CITRUS FRUITS

1 Place a few spoonfuls of apricot jam in a small pan, along with a squeeze of lemon juice. Heat the jam, stirring, until it is melted and runny.

2 Pour the melted jam into a wire sieve set over a bowl. Stir the jam with a wooden spoon to help it go through.

3 Return the strained jam from the bowl to the pan. Keep the glaze warm and brush it generously over the fresh fruit until evenly coated.

1 To grate the rind from a citrus fruit, use the finest side of the grater. Don't remove any of the white pith, and brush off any rind that remains in the grater.

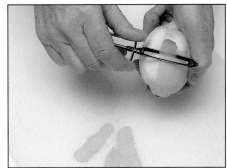

2 To pare the rind from a citrus fruit, use a swivel vegetable peeler. Remove the rind in strips as if peeling a potato, and don't remove any of the white pith.

3 To make citrus rind shreds, or julienne, cut strips of pared rind into very fine shreds using a sharp knife. Boil the shreds for a couple of minutes in water or sugar syrup to soften them.

Low-Fat Whipped "Cream"

Serve this sweet "cream" instead of whipped heavy cream. It isn't suitable for cooking, but it freezes very well.

MAKING LOW-FAT WHIPPED "CREAM"

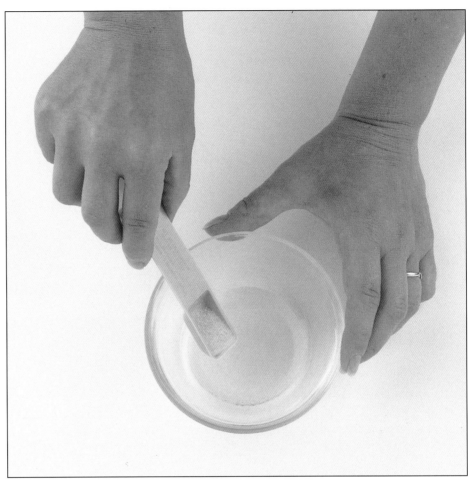

1 Sprinkle ½ teaspoon gelatin over 1 tablespoon cold water in a small bowl and leave to soften for 5 minutes. Place the bowl over a saucepan of hot water and stir until dissolved. Set aside to cool.

2 Whisk ¼ cup skim-milk powder, 1 tablespoon sugar, 1 tablespoon lemon juice and 4 tablespoons cold water until frothy. Add the dissolved gelatin and whisk for a few seconds or more. Chill in the refrigerator for 30 minutes.

3 Whisk the chilled mixture again until very thick and frothy. Serve within 30 minutes of making.

Cook's Tip
Serve strained yogurt with desserts instead of cream, sweetened with a little honey, if you like. Curd cheese can be used instead of cream.

Alternatives to Cream

Yogurt is an excellent alternative to whipped cream for decorating cakes and desserts. Strained yogurt and ricotta cheese are simple to make at home, and tend to be lower in fat than commercial varieties.

MAKING YOGURT PIPING CREAM

1 Sprinkle 2 teaspoons gelatin over 3 tablespoons cold water in a small bowl and let soften for 5 minutes. Place the bowl over a saucepan of hot water and stir until dissolved. Set aside to cool.

2 Mix together 1¼ cups yogurt, 1 tablespoon fructose and ½ teaspoon vanilla extract. Stir in the gelatin. Chill in the refrigerator for 30 minutes.

3 Beat one egg white until stiff and carefully fold it into the yogurt mixture. Spoon into a pastry bag fitted with a piping nozzle and use immediately.

MAKING STRAINED YOGURT AND RICOTTA CHEESE

1 Line a sieve with a double layer of cheesecloth. Put over a bowl and pour in 2½ cups natural low-fat yogurt.

2 Allow to drain in the refrigerator for 3 hours—it will have separated into thick strained yogurt and watery whey.

3 For ricotta cheese, allow to drain in the refrigerator for 8 hours or overnight. Spoon the curd cheese into a bowl, cover and keep chilled until required.

Cakes

Low in fat doesn't have to mean low in taste. These deliciously light cakes are bursting with flavors suited to all seasons and every occasion.

Lemon Chiffon Cake

Lemon mousse provides a tangy filling for this light lemon sponge.

Serves 8
2 eggs
6 tablespoons sugar
grated rind of 1 lemon
½ cup sifted all-purpose flour
shredded lemon rind, to decorate

For the filling
2 eggs, separated
6 tablespoons sugar
grated rind and juice of 1 lemon
½ cup water
1 tablespoon gelatin
½ cup low-fat fromage frais

For the icing
1 tablespoon lemon juice
scant 1 cup confectioners' sugar, sifted

Cook's Tip
The mousse should be just setting when the egg whites are added. Speed up this process by placing the bowl of mousse in iced water.

NUTRITION NOTES
Per portion

Calories	202
Fat	2.81g
Saturated Fat	0.79g
Cholesterol	96.4mg
Fiber	0.2g

1 Preheat the oven to 350°F. Grease and line an 8-inch loose-bottomed cake pan. Beat the eggs, sugar and lemon rind together with a handheld electric mixer until thick and mousselike. Gently fold in the flour, then scrape the mixture into the prepared pan.

2 Bake for 20–25 minutes, until the cake springs back when lightly pressed in the center. Turn onto a wire rack to cool. Once cool, split the cake in half horizontally and return the lower half to the clean cake pan.

3 Make the filling. Put the egg yolks, sugar, lemon rind and juice in a bowl. Beat with a handheld electric mixer until thick, pale and creamy.

4 Pour the water into a heatproof bowl and sprinkle the gelatin on top. Let sit until spongy, then stir over simmering water until dissolved. Cool, then whisk into the yolk mixture. Fold in the fromage frais. When the mixture begins to set, beat the egg whites to soft peaks. Fold the egg whites into the mousse mixture.

5 Pour the lemon mousse over the sponge in the cake pan, spreading it to the edges. Set the second layer of sponge on top and chill until set.

6 Slide an icing spatula dipped in hot water between the pan and the cake to loosen it. Transfer to a serving plate. To make icing, add enough lemon juice to the confectioners' sugar to make a mixture thick enough to coat the back of a wooden spoon. Pour over the cake and spread to the edges. Decorate with shredded lemon rind.

Irish Whiskey Cake

This moist, rich fruit cake is drizzled with whiskey as soon as it comes out of the oven.

Serves 12

4 ounces (⅔ cup) candied cherries
1 cup dark brown sugar
4 ounces (⅔ cup) golden raisins
4 ounces (⅔ cup) raisins
4 ounces (⅔ cup) currants
1¼ cups cold tea
2½ cups self-rising flour, sifted
1 egg
3 tablespoons Irish whiskey

NUTRITION NOTES

Per portion
Calories	265
Fat	0.88g
Saturated Fat	0.25g
Cholesterol	16mg
Fiber	1.48g

1 Mix the cherries, sugar, dried fruit and tea in a large bowl. Let soak overnight, until all the tea has been absorbed into the fruit. Preheat the oven to 350°F.

2 Grease and line a 2¼-pound loaf pan. Add the flour, then the egg to the fruit mixture and beat thoroughly until well mixed.

3 Pour the mixture into the prepared pan and bake for 1½ hours, or until a skewer inserted into the center of the cake comes out clean.

4 Prick the top of the cake with a skewer and drizzle with the whiskey while the cake is still hot. Let stand for about 5 minutes, then remove from the pan and cool on a wire rack.

Cook's Tip
If time is short, use hot tea and soak the fruit for just 2 hours.

Angel Food Cake

A delicious light cake to serve for a special occasion.

1 Preheat the oven to 350°F. Sift the cornstarch and flour onto a sheet of waxed paper.

2 Beat the egg whites in a large clean, dry bowl until very stiff, then gradually add the sugar and vanilla extract, beating until the mixture is thick and glossy.

3 Gently fold in the flour mixture with a large metal spoon. Spoon into an ungreased 10-inch angel food cake pan, smooth the surface and bake for 45–50 minutes, until the cake springs back when lightly pressed.

4 Sprinkle a piece of waxed paper with sugar and set a wine or soda bottle in the center. Invert the cake pan over the paper, balancing it carefully on the neck of the bottle. When cool, the cake will drop out of the pan. Transfer it to a plate, spoon on the glacé icing, arrange the physalis on top, and then dust with confectioners' sugar and serve.

Serves 10

⅓ cup cornstarch
⅓ cup all-purpose flour
8 egg whites
1 cup sugar, plus extra for sprinkling
1 teaspoon vanilla extract
6 tablespoons orange-flavored glacé icing, 4–6 physalis and a little confectioners' sugar, to decorate

NUTRITION NOTES

Per portion

Calories	139
Fat	0.08g
Saturated Fat	0.01g
Cholesterol	0
Fiber	0.13g

Tia Maria Cake

A featherlight coffee sponge with a creamy liqueur-flavored filling.

Serves 8

¾ cup all-purpose flour
2 tablespoons instant coffee granules
3 eggs
½ cup granulated sugar
coffee beans, to decorate (optional)

For the filling

6 ounces (¾ cup) low-fat soft cheese
1 tablespoon honey
1 tablespoon Tia Maria liqueur
2 ounces (¼ cup) preserved ginger,
roughly chopped

For the icing

1¾ cups confectioners' sugar, sifted
2 teaspoons coffee extract
1 tablespoon water
1 teaspoon low-fat cocoa powder

Cook's Tip

When folding in the flour mixture in step 3, be careful not to remove the air, as it helps the cake to rise.

NUTRITION NOTES

Per portion

Calories	226
Fat	3.14g
Saturated Fat	1.17g
Cholesterol	75.03mg
Fiber	0.64g

1 Preheat the oven to 375°F. Grease and line an 8-inch deep round cake pan. Sift the flour and coffee granules together onto a sheet of waxed paper.

2 Beat the eggs and sugar in a bowl with a handheld electric mixer until thick and mousselike. (When the beaters are lifted, a trail should remain on the surface of the mixture for at least 15 seconds.)

3 Gently fold in the flour mixture with a metal spoon. Pour the mixture into the prepared pan. Bake the sponge for 30–35 minutes, or until it springs back when lightly pressed. Turn out onto a wire rack to cool completely.

4 To make the filling, mix the soft cheese with the honey in a bowl. Beat until smooth, then stir in the Tia Maria and chopped preserved ginger.

5 Split the cake in half horizontally and sandwich the two halves together with the Tia Maria filling.

6 Make the icing. In a bowl, mix the confectioners' sugar and coffee extract with enough of the water to create a consistency that will coat the back of a wooden spoon. Pour three-quarters of the icing over the cake, spreading it evenly to the edges. Stir the cocoa into the remaining icing until smooth. Spoon into a pastry bag fitted with a writing nozzle and pipe the mocha icing over the coffee icing. Decorate with coffee beans, if desired.

Chocolate Banana Cake

A chocolate cake that's deliciously low in fat—it is moist enough to eat without the icing
if you want to cut down on calories.

Serves 8

2 cups self-rising flour
3 tablespoons low-fat
cocoa powder
⅔ cup light brown sugar
2 tablespoons malt extract
2 tablespoons golden syrup or
light corn syrup
2 eggs
4 tablespoons skim milk
4 tablespoons sunflower oil
2 large ripe bananas

For the icing

2 cups confectioners' sugar, sifted
7 teaspoons low-fat
cocoa powder, sifted
1–2 tablespoons warm water

NUTRITION NOTES

Per portion
Calories	411
Fat	8.791g
Saturated Fat	2.06g
Cholesterol	48.27mg
Fiber	2.06g

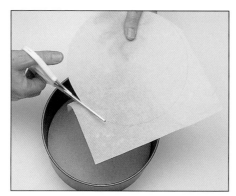

1 Preheat the oven to 325°F. Grease and line a deep round 8-inch cake pan.

2 Sift the flour into a mixing bowl with the cocoa powder. Stir in the sugar.

3 Make a well in the center and add the malt extract, syrup, eggs, milk and oil. Mash the bananas thoroughly and stir them into the mixture until thoroughly combined.

4 Pour the cake mixture into the prepared pan and bake for 1–1¼ hours, or until the center of the cake springs back when lightly pressed.

5 Remove the cake from the pan and leave on a wire rack to cool.

6 Reserve ⅓ cup confectioners' sugar and 1 teaspoon cocoa powder. Make a dark icing by beating the remaining sugar and cocoa powder with enough of the warm water to make a thick icing. Pour it over the top of the cake and spread evenly to the edges. Make a thinner, lighter icing by mixing the reserved sugar and cocoa powder with a few drops of water. Drizzle or pipe this icing across the top of the cake to decorate.

Coffee Sponge Drops

These are delicious on their own, but taste even better with a filling made by mixing low-fat soft cheese with drained and chopped preserved ginger.

Makes 12
½ cup all-purpose flour
1 tablespoon instant coffee granules
2 eggs
6 tablespoons sugar

For the filling
4 ounces (½ cup) low-fat soft cheese
1½ ounces (¼ cup) chopped preserved ginger

1 Preheat the oven to 375°F. Line two baking sheets with baking parchment. Make the filling by beating together the soft cheese and ginger. Chill until required. Sift the flour and instant coffee granules together.

3 Carefully add the sifted flour and coffee mixture and gently fold in with a metal spoon, being careful not to knock out any air.

2 Combine the eggs and sugar in a bowl. Beat with a handheld electric mixer until thick and mousselike. (When the beaters are lifted, a trail should remain on the surface of the mixture for at least 15 seconds.)

4 Spoon the mixture into a pastry bag fitted with a ½-inch plain nozzle. Pipe 1½-inch rounds on the baking sheets. Bake for 12 minutes. Cool on a wire rack, then sandwich together with the filling.

Cook's Tip
As an alternative to preserved ginger in the filling, try walnuts.

NUTRITION NOTES
Per portion

Calories	69
Fat	1.36g
Saturated Fat	0.5g
Cholesterol	33.33mg
Fiber	0.29g

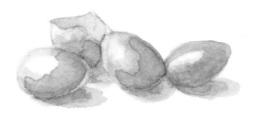

Chocolate-Orange Angel Food Cake

This light-as-air sponge with its fluffy icing is virtually fat free, yet tastes heavenly.

Serves 10

¼ cup all-purpose flour
2 tablespoons low-fat
cocoa powder
2 tablespoons cornstarch
pinch of salt
5 egg whites
½ teaspoon cream of tartar
scant ½ cup sugar
blanched and shredded rind of
1 orange, to decorate

For the icing

1 cup sugar
1 egg white

1 Preheat the oven to 350°F. Sift the flour, cocoa powder, cornstarch and salt together three times. Beat the egg whites in a large clean, dry bowl until foamy. Add the cream of tartar, then beat until soft peaks form.

2 Add the sugar to the egg whites a spoonful at a time, beating after each addition. Sift a third of the flour and cocoa mixture over the meringue and gently fold in. Repeat, sifting and folding in the flour and cocoa mixture two more times.

3 Spoon the mixture into a nonstick 8-inch ring mold and level the top. Bake for 35 minutes, or until springy to the touch. Turn upside down onto a wire rack and let cool in the pan. Carefully ease out of the pan.

4 For the icing, put the sugar in a pan with 5 tablespoons cold water. Stir over low heat until dissolved. Boil until the syrup reaches a temperature of 240°F on a candy thermometer or when a drop of the syrup makes a soft ball when dripped into a cup of cold water. Remove from the heat.

5 Beat the egg white until stiff. Add the syrup in a thin stream, beating constantly. Continue to beat until the mixture is very thick and fluffy.

6 Spread the icing over the top and sides of the cooled cake. Sprinkle the orange rind over the top of the cake and serve.

NUTRITION NOTES

Per portion	
Calories	53
Fat	0.27g
Saturated Fat	0.13g
Cholesterol	0
Fiber	0.25g

Apricot and Orange Roulade

This elegant dessert is very good served with a spoonful of plain yogurt or crème fraîche.

Serves 6

4 egg whites
½ cup raw sugar
½ cup all-purpose flour
finely grated rind of 1 small orange
3 tablespoons orange juice
2 teaspoons confectioners' sugar and
orange zest, to decorate

For the filling
4 ounces (⅔ cup) dried apricots
⅔ cup orange juice

NUTRITION NOTES

Per portion

Calories	203
Fat	10.52g
Saturated Fat	2.05g
Cholesterol	0
Fiber	2.53g

1 Preheat the oven to 400°F. Grease a 9 x 13-inch jelly roll pan and line it with baking parchment. Grease the paper.

2 For the roulade, place the egg whites in a large bowl and beat them until they hold peaks. Gradually add the sugar, beating hard between each addition.

3 Fold in the flour, orange rind and juice. Spoon the mixture into the prepared pan and spread it evenly.

4 Bake for about 15–18 minutes, or until the sponge is firm and light golden in color. Turn out onto a sheet of baking parchment and loosely roll it up jelly-roll-style from one short side. Allow to cool.

5 For the filling, roughly chop the apricots and place them in a saucepan with the orange juice. Cover the pan and let simmer until most of the liquid has been absorbed. Purée the apricots in a food processor or blender.

6 Unroll the roulade and spread with the apricot mixture. Roll up, arrange strips of paper diagonally across the roll, sprinkle lightly with lines of confectioners' sugar, remove the paper and sprinkle with orange zest to serve.

Cook's Tip
Make and bake the sponge mixture a day in advance and keep it, rolled with the paper, in a cool place. Fill it with the fruit purée 2–3 hours before serving. The sponge can also be frozen for up to 2 months; thaw it at room temperature and fill it as above.

Nectarine Amaretto Cake

Amaretto liqueur adds a hint of luxury to this fruity cake.

1 Preheat the oven to 350°F. Grease an 8-inch round loose-bottomed cake pan. Beat together the egg yolks, sugar, lemon rind and juice in a bowl until the mixture is thick, pale and creamy.

2 Fold in the semolina, almonds and flour until smooth.

3 Beat the egg whites in a bowl until fairly stiff. Use a metal spoon to stir a generous spoonful of the whites into the semolina mixture, then fold in the remaining egg whites. Spoon the mixture into the cake pan.

4 Bake for 30–35 minutes, until the center of the cake springs back when pressed lightly. Remove from the oven and loosen around the edge with a metal spatula. Prick the top all over with a skewer. Allow to cool in the pan.

5 To make the syrup, heat the sugar and water in a small pan, stirring until the sugar is dissolved. Boil without stirring for 2 minutes. Add the Amaretto liqueur and drizzle the liqueur syrup over the cake in the pan.

6 Remove the cake from the pan and transfer to a serving plate. Decorate with sliced nectarines. Brush with warm apricot glaze.

Serves 8

3 eggs, separated
¾ cup sugar
grated rind and juice of 1 lemon
⅓ cup semolina
¼ cup ground almonds
¼ cup all-purpose flour
2 nectarines, pitted and sliced
4 tablespoons apricot glaze

For the syrup

⅓ cup sugar
6 tablespoons water
2 tablespoons Amaretto liqueur

NUTRITION NOTES

Per portion	
Calories	264
Fat	5.7g
Saturated Fat	0.85g
Cholesterol	72.19mg
Fiber	1.08g

Banana and Gingerbread Slices

Very quick to make and deliciously moist due to the addition of bananas.

Serves 20

2 cups all-purpose flour
4 teaspoons ground ginger
2 teaspoons apple pie spice
1 teaspoon baking soda
½ cup light brown sugar
4 tablespoons sunflower oil
2 tablespoons molasses
2 tablespoons malt extract
2 eggs
4 tablespoons orange juice
3 bananas
4 ounces (⅔ cup) raisins

Variation

To make Spiced Honey and Banana Cake; omit the ground ginger and add another 1 teaspoon apple pie spice; omit the malt extract and the molasses and add 4 tablespoons strong-flavored honey instead; and replace the raisins with either golden raisins, coarsely chopped dried apricots, or semi-dried pineapple. If you choose to use the pineapple, then you could also replace the orange juice with fresh pineapple juice.

Cook's Tip

The flavor of this cake develops as it keeps, so if you can, store it for a few days before eating.

NUTRITION NOTES

Per portion

Calories	148
Fat	3.07g
Saturated Fat	0.53g
Cholesterol	19.3mg
Fiber	0.79g

1 Preheat the oven to 350°F. Lightly grease and line a 7 x 11-inch baking pan.

2 Sift the flour into a bowl with the spices and baking soda. Mix the sugar with some of the flour and sift it all into the bowl.

3 Make a well in the center, add the oil, molasses, malt extract, eggs and orange juice and mix together thoroughly.

4 Mash the bananas, then add them to the bowl with the raisins and mix together well.

5 Pour the mixture into the prepared baking pan and bake for 35–40 minutes, or until the center springs back when lightly pressed.

6 Leave the cake in the pan to cool for 5 minutes, then turn out onto a wire rack and allow to cool completely. Cut into 20 slices.

Banana-Oatmeal Gingerbread

This gingerbread keeps well and really improves over time; it can be stored for up to two months.

Serves 12

1¾ cups all-purpose flour
2 teaspoons baking soda
2 teaspoons ground ginger
1¾ cups rolled oats
4 tablespoons dark brown sugar
6 tablespoons sunflower margarine
⅔ cup golden syrup or light corn syrup
1 egg, beaten
3 ripe bananas, mashed
¾ cup confectioners' sugar
preserved ginger, to decorate

NUTRITION NOTES

Per portion

Calories	277
Fat	6.9g
Saturated Fat	6.9g
Cholesterol	16.4mg
Fiber	1.72g

1 Preheat the oven to 325°F. Grease and line a 7 x 11-inch cake pan.

2 Sift together the flour, baking soda and ginger, then stir in the oats. Melt the sugar, margarine and syrup in a saucepan, then stir into the flour mixture. Beat in the egg and mashed bananas.

3 Spoon into the pan and bake for about 1 hour, or until firm to the touch. Allow to cool in the pan, then turn out and cut into squares.

4 Sift the confectioners' sugar into a bowl and stir in just enough water to make a smooth, runny icing. Drizzle the icing over each square and top with a piece of preserved ginger, to decorate.

Cook's Tip

This is a nutritious, energy-giving cake that is a good choice for brown-bag lunches because it doesn't break up easily.

Spiced Date and Walnut Cake

A classic flavor combination that makes a very easy low-fat, high-fiber cake.

1 Preheat the oven to 350°F. Grease and line a 2-pound loaf pan with waxed paper.

2 Sift together the flour, baking powder, salt and spice, returning any bran from the sieve. Stir in the dates and walnuts.

3 Mix the oil, sugar and milk, then stir evenly into the dry ingredients.

4 Spoon into the prepared pan and arrange the walnut halves on top. Bake the cake in the oven for 45–50 minutes, or until golden brown and firm. Turn out the cake, remove the lining paper and let cool on a wire rack.

Serves 10

2½ cups whole-wheat flour
4 teaspoons baking powder
½ teaspoon salt
2 teaspoons apple pie spice
5 ounces (¾ cup) chopped dates
2 ounces (½ cup) chopped walnuts
4 tablespoons sunflower oil
½ cup dark brown sugar
1¼ cups skim milk
walnut halves, to decorate

NUTRITION NOTES

Per portion

Calories	265
Fat	9.27g
Saturated Fat	1.14g
Cholesterol	0.6mg
Fiber	3.51g

Cook's Tip

Pecans can be used in place of the walnuts in this cake.

Greek Honey and Lemon Cake

Moist and tangy, a delicious afternoon snack.

Makes 16 slices

3 tablespoons sunflower margarine
4 tablespoons honey
finely grated rind and juice of 1 lemon
⅔ cup skim milk
1¼ cups all-purpose flour
1½ teaspoons baking powder
½ teaspoon grated nutmeg
¼ cup semolina
2 egg whites
2 teaspoons sesame seeds

NUTRITION NOTES

Per portion

Calories	82
Fat	2.62g
Saturated Fat	0.46g
Cholesterol	0.36mg
Fiber	0.41g

1 Preheat the oven to 400°F. Lightly oil a 7½-inch square deep cake pan and line the bottom with baking parchment.

2 Place the margarine and 3 tablespoons of the honey in a saucepan and heat gently until melted. Reserve 1 tablespoon lemon juice, then stir in the rest with the lemon rind and milk.

3 Sift together the flour, baking powder and nutmeg. Gradually beat the semolina into the mixture. Beat the egg whites until they form soft peaks, then fold evenly into the mixture.

4 Spoon into the pan and sprinkle with sesame seeds. Bake for 25–30 minutes, until golden brown. Mix together the reserved honey and lemon juice and drizzle over the cake while warm. Cool in the pan, then cut into fingers to serve.

Strawberry Roulade

A creamy fruit filling is delicious in a light roulade.

1 Preheat the oven to 400°F. Oil a 9 x 13-inch jelly roll pan and line with baking parchment.

2 Place the egg whites in a large bowl and beat until they form soft peaks. Gradually beat in the sugar. Fold in half of the sifted flour, then fold in the rest with the orange juice.

3 Spoon the mixture into the prepared pan, spreading evenly. Bake for 15–18 minutes, or until golden brown and firm to the touch.

4 Meanwhile, spread out a sheet of baking parchment and sprinkle with granulated sugar. Turn out the cake onto this and remove the lining paper. Roll up the sponge loosely from one short side, with the paper inside. Cool.

5 Unroll and remove the paper. Stir the strawberries into the fromage frais and spread over the sponge. Re-roll and serve decorated with strawberries.

Serves 6

4 egg whites
⅔ cup raw sugar
⅔ cup all-purpose flour, sifted
2 tablespoons orange juice
granulated sugar, for sprinkling
4 ounces (1 cup) strawberries, chopped
5 ounces (¾ cup) low-fat fromage frais
strawberries, to decorate

NUTRITION NOTES
Per portion

Calories	154
Fat	0.24g
Saturated Fat	0.01g
Cholesterol	0.25mg
Fiber	0.61g

Peach Jelly Roll

A featherlight sponge enclosing peach jam—delicious with tea.

Serves 6–8
3 eggs
½ cup granulated sugar, plus extra
for sprinkling
¾ cup all-purpose flour, sifted
1 tablespoon boiling water
6 tablespoons peach jam
confectioners' sugar, for dusting
(optional)

Cook's Tip
To decorate the jelly roll with glacé icing, make the icing with 1¾ cups confectioners' sugar and enough warm water to make a thin glacé icing. Put in a pastry bag fitted with a small writing nozzle and pipe lines over the top.

NUTRITION NOTES
Per portion
Calories	178
Fat	2.54g
Saturated Fat	0.67g
Cholesterol	82.5mg
Fiber	0.33g

1 Preheat the oven to 400°F. Grease a 12 x 8-inch jelly roll pan and line with baking parchment. Combine the eggs and sugar in a bowl. Beat with a hand-held electric mixer until thick and mousselike. (When the beaters are lifted, a trail should remain on the surface of the mixture for at least 15 seconds.)

2 Carefully fold in the flour with a large metal spoon, then add the boiling water in the same way.

3 Spoon into the prepared pan, spread evenly to the edges and bake for 10–12 minutes, until the cake springs back when lightly pressed.

4 Spread a sheet of waxed paper on a flat surface, sprinkle it with granulated sugar, then invert the cake on top. Peel off the lining paper.

5 Neatly trim the edges of the cake. Make a neat cut two-thirds of the way through the cake, about ½ inch from the short edge nearest you.

6 Spread the cake with the peach jam and roll up quickly from the partially cut end. Hold in position for a minute, making sure the seam is underneath. Cool on a wire rack. Decorate with glacé icing (see Cook's Tip) or dust with confectioners' sugar before serving.

Spiced Apple Cake

Grated apple and chopped dates give this cake a natural sweetness.

Serves 8

2 cups whole-wheat flour
4 teaspoons baking powder
¼ teaspoon salt
2 teaspoons ground cinnamon
6 ounces (1 cup) chopped dates
½ cup light brown sugar
1 tablespoon pear and apple spread
½ cup apple juice
2 eggs
6 tablespoons sunflower oil
2 eating apples, cored and grated
1 tablespoon chopped walnuts

NUTRITION NOTES

Per portion
Calories	331
Fat	11.41g
Saturated Fat	1.68g
Cholesterol	48.13mg
Fiber	2.5g

1 Preheat the oven to 350°F. Grease and line a deep round 8-inch cake pan. Sift the flour, baking powder, salt and cinnamon into a mixing bowl, then mix in the dates and make a well in the center.

2 Mix the sugar with the pear and apple spread in a small bowl. Gradually stir in the apple juice. Add to the dry ingredients with the eggs, oil and grated apples. Mix thoroughly.

3 Spoon the mixture into the prepared cake pan, sprinkle with the walnuts and bake for 60–65 minutes, or until a skewer inserted into the center of the cake comes out clean. Transfer to a wire rack, remove the lining paper and allow to cool.

Cook's Tip
Omit 2 tablespoons sugar if the fruit is very sweet. It is not necessary to peel the apples—the skin adds extra fiber and softens when cooked.

Fruit and Nut Cake

A rich fruit cake that improves with keeping.

1 Preheat the oven to 325°F. Grease and line a deep round 8-inch cake pan. Secure a band of brown paper around the outside.

2 Sift the flours, baking powder, salt and spice into a mixing bowl and make a well in the center.

3 Put the apple and apricot spread in a small bowl. Gradually stir in the honey and molasses. Add to the dry ingredients with the oil, orange juice, eggs and mixed fruit. Mix thoroughly.

4 Turn the mixture into the prepared pan and smooth the surface. Arrange the almonds and cherries in a pattern over the top. Bake for 2 hours, or until a skewer inserted into the center comes out clean. Transfer to a wire rack and let cool, then lift out of the pan and remove the paper.

Serves 12–14

1½ cups whole-wheat flour
1½ cups self-rising white flour
2¼ teaspoons baking powder
¼ teaspoon salt
2 teaspoons apple pie spice
1 tablespoon apple and apricot spread
3 tablespoons honey
1 tablespoon molasses
6 tablespoons sunflower oil
¾ cup orange juice
2 eggs, beaten
1½ pounds (4 cups) deluxe mixed dried fruit
3 tablespoons blanched almonds
2 ounces (½ cup) candied cherries, halved

NUTRITION NOTES

Per portion	
Calories	333
Fat	8.54g
Saturated Fat	1.12g
Cholesterol	29.62mg
Fiber	3.08g

Eggless Christmas Cake

A deliciously clever way to create a low-calorie Christmas treat!

Serves 12

½ cup golden raisins
½ cup raisins
⅔ cup currants
½ cup candied cherries, halved
⅓ cup cut mixed peel
1 cup apple juice
¼ cup toasted hazelnuts
2 tablespoons pumpkin seeds
2 pieces preserved ginger
in syrup, chopped
finely grated rind of 1 lemon
½ cup skim milk
½ cup sunflower oil
2 cups whole-wheat flour
4 teaspoons baking powder
¼ teaspoon salt
2 teaspoons apple pie spice
3 tablespoons brandy or dark rum
apricot jam, for brushing
candied fruits, to decorate

1 Place the golden raisins, raisins, currants, cherries and mixed peel in a bowl and stir in the apple juice. Cover and allow to soak overnight.

2 Preheat the oven to 300°F.

3 Lightly grease and line a 7-inch square cake pan.

4 Add the nuts, seeds, ginger and rind to the soaked fruit. Stir in the milk and oil. Sift the flour, baking powder, salt, and spice. Stir in with the brandy or rum.

5 Spoon into the prepared pan and bake for 1½ hours, or until golden brown and firm to the touch. Turn out and cool on a wire rack. Brush with sieved apricot jam and decorate with candied fruits.

NUTRITION NOTES

Per portion

Calories	225
Fat	6.13g
Saturated Fat	0.89g
Cholesterol	0.2mg
Fiber	2.45g

Cranberry and Apple Ring

Tangy cranberries add an unusual flavor to this low-fat cake. It is best eaten very fresh.

1 Preheat the oven to 350°F. Lightly grease a 4-cup ring mold with oil.

2 Sift together the flour and ground cinnamon, then stir in the sugar.

3 Toss together the diced apple and cranberries. Stir into the dry ingredients, then add the oil and apple juice and beat well.

4 Spoon the mixture into the prepared ring mold and bake for 35–40 minutes, or until the cake is firm to the touch. Turn out and let cool completely on a wire rack.

5 To serve, drizzle warmed cranberry jelly over the top and decorate with apple slices.

Serves 8

2 cups self-rising flour
1 teaspoon ground cinnamon
½ cup light brown sugar
1 crisp eating apple, cored and diced
3 ounces (½ cup) fresh or
frozen cranberries
4 tablespoons sunflower oil
⅔ cup apple juice
cranberry jelly and apple slices,
to decorate

NUTRITION NOTES

Per portion

Calories	202
Fat	5.91g
Saturated Fat	0.76g
Cholesterol	0
Fiber	1.55g

Cook's Tip

Fresh cranberries are available throughout the winter months and if you don't use them all at once, they can be frozen for up to a year.

Carrot Cake with Lemon Frosting

Lemon frosting is the perfect topping for this all-time favorite.

Serves 8

2 cups whole-wheat flour
3 teaspoons baking powder
¼ teaspoon salt
2 teaspoons ground allspice
⅔ cup light brown sugar
2 medium carrots, grated
2 ounces (⅓ cup) golden raisins
5 tablespoons sunflower oil
5 tablespoons orange juice
5 tablespoons skim milk
2 egg whites

For the frosting

¾ cup skim-milk soft cheese
finely grated rind of ½ lemon
2 tablespoons honey
shredded lemon rind, to decorate

NUTRITION NOTES

Per portion
Calories	272
Fat	7.72g
Saturated Fat	1.04g
Cholesterol	0.4mg
Fiber	3.33g

1 Preheat the oven to 350°F. Grease a deep 7-inch round cake pan and line the bottom with baking parchment.

2 Sift together the flour, baking powder, salt and spice, then stir in the sugar, grated carrots and golden raisins.

3 Mix the liquids, then stir into the dry ingredients. Beat the egg whites until stiff, then fold in evenly. Spoon into the pan and bake for 45–50 minutes.

4 Turn out and let cool. For the frosting, beat together the cheese, lemon rind and honey until smooth. Spread over the top of the cooled cake, swirling with an icing spatula. Decorate with lemon rind.

Chewy Fruit Muesli Slice

Low in fat and high in fiber . . . and delicious as well.

1 Preheat the oven to 375°F. Place all the ingredients in a large bowl and mix well. Press the mixture into an 8-inch round nonstick layer-cake pan and bake for 35–40 minutes, or until lightly browned and firm.

2 Mark the muesli slice into wedges and allow to cool in the pan.

Makes 8 slices

3 ounces (½ cup) dried apricots, chopped
1 eating apple, cored and grated
5 ounces (1¼ cups) Swiss-style muesli
⅔ cup apple juice
1 tablespoon soft sunflower margarine

NUTRITION NOTES

Per portion

Calories	112
Fat	2.75g
Saturated Fat	0.48g
Cholesterol	0.13mg
Fiber	2.09g

Ginger Cake with Spiced Cream

A spicy and comforting cake, ideal for winter evenings.

Serves 9

1½ cups all-purpose flour
2 teaspoons baking powder
½ teaspoon salt
2 teaspoons ground ginger
2 teaspoons ground cinnamon
1 teaspoon ground cloves
¼ teaspoon ground nutmeg
2 eggs
1 cup granulated sugar
1 cup whipping cream
1 teaspoon vanilla extract
confectioners' sugar, to decorate

For the spiced whipped cream

¾ cup whipping cream
1 teaspoon confectioners' sugar
¼ teaspoon ground cinnamon
¼ teaspoon ground ginger
⅛ teaspoon grated nutmeg

1 Preheat the oven to 350°F. Grease a 9-inch square baking pan.

2 Sift the flour, baking powder, salt, ginger, cinnamon, cloves and nutmeg into a bowl. Set aside.

3 With an electric mixer, beat the eggs on high speed until very thick, about 5 minutes. Gradually beat in the granulated sugar.

4 With the mixer on low speed, beat in the flour mixture alternately with the cream into the eggs, beginning and ending with the flour. Stir in the vanilla.

5 Pour into the pan and bake until the top springs back when touched lightly, 35–40 minutes. Allow to cool in the pan on a wire rack for 10 minutes.

6 To make the spiced whipped cream, combine the ingredients in a bowl and whip until the cream holds soft peaks. Sprinkle confectioners' sugar over the hot cake, cut into nine squares and serve with the spiced whipped cream.

NUTRITION NOTES

Per portion

Calories	305
Fat	11.6g
Saturated Fat	6.6g
Cholesterol	69mg
Fiber	0.8g

Apple and Pear Skillet Cake

An unusual but delicious cake, prepared on the stove and then baked in the oven.

1 Preheat the oven to 375°F. In a mixing bowl, toss together the apple slices, pear slices, walnuts, cinnamon and nutmeg. Set aside.

2 With an electric mixer, beat together the eggs, flour, brown sugar, milk and vanilla.

3 Melt the butter or margarine in a 9- or 10-inch ovenproof skillet (preferably cast iron) over medium heat. Add the apple mixture. Cook until lightly caramelized, about 5 minutes, stirring occasionally.

4 Pour the batter over the fruit and nuts. Transfer the skillet to the oven and bake for about 30 minutes, until the cake is puffy and pulling away from the sides of the pan.

5 Sprinkle the cake lightly with confectioners' sugar and serve hot.

Serves 6

1 apple, peeled, cored and thinly sliced
1 pear, peeled, cored and thinly sliced
2 ounces (½ cup) walnuts, chopped
1 teaspoon ground cinnamon
1 teaspoon grated nutmeg
3 eggs
¾ cup all-purpose flour
2 tablespoons light brown sugar, firmly packed
¾ cup skim milk
1 teaspoon vanilla extract
4 tablespoons butter or margarine
confectioners' sugar, for sprinkling

NUTRITION NOTES

Per portion

Calories	315
Fat	19.9g
Saturated Fat	3.3g
Cholesterol	98mg
Fiber	1.8g

Cinnamon Apple Cake

Make this lovely cake for an autumn celebration.

Serves 6
3 eggs
½ cup sugar
¾ cup all-purpose flour
1 teaspoon ground cinnamon

For the filling and topping
4 large eating apples
4 tablespoons honey
½ cup golden raisins
½ teaspoon ground cinnamon
12 ounces low-fat soft cheese
4 tablespoons reduced-fat
fromage frais
2 teaspoons lemon juice
3 tablespoons apricot glaze
mint sprigs, to decorate

Cook's Tip
Apricot glaze is useful for brushing over a fresh fruit top-ping or filling. Place a few spoonfuls of apricot jam in a small pan along with a squeeze of lemon juice. Heat the jam, stirring until it is melted and runny. Pour the melted jam into a wire sieve set over a bowl. Stir the jam with a wooden spoon to help it go through. Return the strained jam to the pan. Keep the glaze warm until needed.

NUTRITION NOTES
Per portion

Calories	203
Fat	10.52g
Saturated Fat	2.05g
Cholesterol	77mg
Fiber	2.53g

1 Preheat the oven to 375°F. Grease and line a 9-inch layer-cake pan. Place the eggs and sugar in a bowl and beat with a handheld electric mixer until thick and mousselike. (When the beaters are lifted, a trail should remain on the surface of the mixture for at least 15 seconds.)

2 Sift the flour and cinnamon over the egg mixture and fold in with a large metal spoon. Pour into the prepared pan and bake for 25–30 minutes, or until the cake springs back when lightly pressed. Turn out onto a wire rack to cool.

3 To make the filling, peel, core and slice three of the apples and put them in a saucepan. Add 2 tablespoons of the honey and 1 tablespoon water. Cover and cook over gentle heat for about 10 minutes. Add the golden raisins and cinnamon, stir well, replace the lid and allow to cool.

4 Put the soft cheese in a bowl with the remaining honey, the fromage frais and half the lemon juice. Beat until the mixture is smooth.

5 Halve the cake horizontally, place the bottom half on a board and drizzle any liquid from the apples over it. Spread with two-thirds of the cheese mixture, then top with the apple filling. Fit the top of the cake in place.

6 Swirl the remaining cheese mixture over the top of the cake. Core and slice the remaining apple, sprinkle with lemon juice and use to decorate the edge of the cake. Brush the apple slices with the apricot glaze and place mint sprigs on top, to decorate.

Scones,
Muffins,
Buns and
Cookies

Served warm and straight
from the oven, these
small treats are a
pleasure for the palate—
with the added health
benefit of a reduced-fat
content.

Blueberry Muffins

An old favorite—and they are not high in calories or fat.

Makes 12

1¼ cups all-purpose flour

⅓ cup sugar

2 teaspoons baking powder

½ teaspoon salt

2 eggs

4 tablespoons butter, melted

¾ cup skim milk

1 teaspoon vanilla extract

1 teaspoon grated lemon rind

4 ounces (1 cup) fresh blueberries

NUTRITION NOTES

Per portion

Calories	124
Fat	3.9g
Saturated Fat	0.8g
Cholesterol	33mg
Fiber	0.8g

1 Preheat the oven to 400°F.

2 Grease a 12-cup muffin pan or use paper liners.

3 Sift the flour, sugar, baking powder and salt into a bowl.

4 In another bowl, beat the eggs until blended. Add the melted butter, milk, vanilla extract and lemon rind and stir to combine. Make a well in the dry ingredients and pour in the egg mixture. With a large metal spoon, stir just until the flour is moistened, not until smooth.

5 Fold in the blueberries.

6 Spoon the batter into the cups, leaving room for the muffins to rise. Bake for 20–25 minutes, or until well risen and firm in the middle. Allow to cool in the pan for about 5 minutes before turning out.

Apple Cranberry Muffins

Fruit and nuts are a winning combination in these mouthwatering muffins.

1 Preheat the oven to 350°F. Grease a 12-cup muffin pan or use paper liners.

2 Melt the butter or margarine over gentle heat. Set aside to cool.

3 Place the egg in a mixing bowl and beat lightly. Add the melted butter or margarine and beat to combine.

4 Add the sugar, orange rind and juice. Beat to blend, then set aside. In a large bowl, sift together the flour, baking powder, baking soda, cinnamon, nutmeg, allspice, ginger and salt. Set aside.

5 Quarter, core and peel the apples. Then dice coarsely, using a sharp knife.

6 Make a well in the dry ingredients and pour in the egg mixture. With a spoon, stir until just blended. Add the apples, cranberries and walnuts and stir to blend.

7 Fill the muffin cups three-quarters full and bake for 25–30 minutes, or until well risen and firm in the middle. Transfer the muffins to a rack to cool. Dust lightly with confectioners' sugar before serving.

Makes 12

4 tablespoons butter or margarine
1 egg
½ cup granulated sugar
grated rind of 1 large orange
½ cup fresh orange juice
½ cup all-purpose flour
½ teaspoon baking powder
½ teaspoon baking soda
1 teaspoon ground cinnamon
½ teaspoon grated nutmeg
2½ teaspoons ground allspice
¼ teaspoon ginger
¼ teaspoon salt
1–2 eating apples
4 ounces (1 cup) cranberries
2 ounces (½ cup) walnuts, chopped
confectioners' sugar, for dusting

NUTRITION NOTES

Per portion

Calories	175
Fat	9.1g
Saturated Fat	1.4g
Cholesterol	16mg
Fiber	1.4g

Raspberry Muffins

These muffins are made using baking powder and low-fat buttermilk, giving them a light and spongy texture. They are delicious to eat at any time of the day.

Makes 10–12
2½ cups all-purpose flour
1 tablespoon baking powder
½ cup sugar
1 egg
1 cup buttermilk
4 tablespoons sunflower oil
5 ounces (1 cup) raspberries

NUTRITION NOTES
Per portion
Calories	171
Fat	4.55g
Saturated Fat	0.71g
Cholesterol	16.5mg
Fiber	1.02g

1 Preheat the oven to 400°F. Grease a 12-cup muffin pan or use paper liners. Sift the flour and baking powder into a mixing bowl, stir in the sugar, then make a well in the center.

2 Mix the egg, buttermilk and sunflower oil together in a bowl, pour into the flour mixture and mix quickly.

3 Add the raspberries and lightly fold in with a metal spoon. Spoon the mixture into the pan or paper liners.

4 Bake the muffins for 20–25 minutes, until golden brown and firm in the middle. Transfer to a wire rack and serve warm or cool.

Spiced Banana Muffins

These light and nutritious muffins include banana for added fiber and make a tasty afternoon treat.
If desired, slice off the tops and fill with jam.

1 Preheat the oven to 400°F. Grease a 12-cup muffin pan or use paper liners. Sift together both flours, the baking powder, salt and apple pie spice into a bowl, then tip the bran remaining in the sieve into the bowl. Stir in the sugar.

2 Melt the margarine and pour it into a mixing bowl. Cool slightly, then beat in the egg, milk and grated orange rind.

3 Gently fold in the dry ingredients. Mash the banana with a fork, then stir it gently into the mixture, being careful not to overmix.

4 Spoon the mixture into the greased pan or paper liners. Combine the oats and hazelnuts and sprinkle a little of the mixture over each muffin.

5 Bake in the preheated oven for 20 minutes, until the muffins are well risen and golden and a skewer inserted in the center comes out clean. Transfer to a wire rack and allow to cool. These muffins can be served warm or cold.

Makes 12
¾ cup whole-wheat flour
½ cup all-purpose flour
2 teaspoons baking powder
pinch of salt
1 teaspoon apple pie spice
¼ cup light brown sugar, firmly packed
¼ cup polyunsaturated margarine
1 egg, beaten
⅔ cup low-fat milk
grated rind of 1 orange
1 ripe banana
¼ cup rolled oats
¾ ounce (scant ¼ cup) chopped hazelnuts

NUTRITION NOTES
Per portion

Calories	139
Fat	0.08g
Saturated Fat	0.1g
Cholesterol	0
Fiber	0.13g

Carrot Muffins

Moist and full of flavor, these unusual muffins are a must.

Makes 12

12 tablespoons (1½ sticks) margarine,
at room temperature
½ cup dark brown sugar,
firmly packed
1 egg, at room temperature
1 tablespoon water
5 ounces (2 cups) grated carrot
1¼ cups all-purpose flour
1 teaspoon baking powder
½ teaspoon baking soda
1 teaspoon ground cinnamon
¼ teaspoon grated nutmeg
½ teaspoon salt

NUTRITION NOTES

Per portion

Calories	155
Fat	9.2g
Saturated Fat	1.8g
Cholesterol	13mg
Fiber	0.8g

1 Preheat the oven to 350°F. Grease a 12-cup muffin pan or use paper liners.

2 With an electric mixer, cream the margarine and sugar until they are light and fluffy. Beat in the egg and water. Stir in the carrot.

3 Sift over the flour, baking powder, baking soda, cinnamon, nutmeg and salt. Stir to blend.

4 Spoon the batter into the prepared muffin cups, filling them almost to the top. Bake for about 35 minutes, until well risen and firm in the middle. Allow to stand for 10 minutes before transferring to a rack.

Dried Cherry Muffins

Muffins make a wonderful breakfast, particularly on special occasions.

1 In a mixing bowl, combine the yogurt and cherries. Cover and let stand for 30 minutes. Preheat the oven to 350°F. Grease 16 muffin cups or use paper liners.

2 With an electric mixer, cream the butter and sugar together until they are light and fluffy.

3 Add the eggs, one at a time, beating well after each addition.

4 Add the vanilla extract and the cherry mixture and stir to blend. Set aside. In another bowl, sift together the flour, baking powder, baking soda and salt. Fold into the cherry mixture in three batches; do not overmix.

5 Fill the prepared muffin cups two-thirds full. For even baking, half-fill any empty cups with water. Bake for about 20 minutes, or until well risen and firm in the middle. Transfer to a rack.

Makes 16

8 ounces (1 cup) plain yogurt
8 ounces (1 cup) dried cherries
8 tablespoons (1 stick) butter, at room temperature
¾ cup sugar
2 eggs, at room temperature
1 teaspoon vanilla extract
1¾ cups all-purpose flour
2 teaspoons baking powder
1 teaspoon baking soda
⅛ teaspoon salt

NUTRITION NOTES

Per portion

Calories	197
Fat	6.8g
Saturated Fat	1.4g
Cholesterol	25mg
Fiber	0.7g

Oatmeal Buttermilk Muffins

Add a Scottish flavor to your afternoon snacks.

Makes 12

1 cup rolled oats
1 cup buttermilk
8 tablespoons (1 stick) butter, at room temperature
½ cup dark brown sugar, firmly packed
1 egg, at room temperature
1 cup all-purpose flour
1 teaspoon baking powder
½ teaspoon salt
1 ounce (¼ cup) raisins

NUTRITION NOTES

Per portion

Calories	213
Fat	9.3g
Saturated Fat	1.9g
Cholesterol	17mg
Fiber	1.2g

1 In a bowl, combine the oats and buttermilk and allow to soak for 1 hour.

2 Grease a 12-cup muffin pan or use paper liners.

3 Preheat the oven to 400°F. With an electric mixer, cream the butter and sugar until light and fluffy. Beat in the egg.

4 In another bowl, sift together the flour, baking powder and salt. Stir the dry ingredients into the butter mixture, alternating with the oat mixture. Fold in the raisins, taking care not to overmix.

5 Fill the prepared cups two-thirds full. Bake for 20–25 minutes, until a cake tester or skewer inserted in the center comes out clean. Transfer to a wire rack to cool.

Pumpkin Muffins

Pumpkin has a mild, sweet flavor and makes a delicious, moist muffin.

1 Preheat the oven to 400°F. Grease 14 muffin cups or use paper liners. With an electric mixer, cream the butter or margarine until soft. Add the sugar and molasses and beat until light and fluffy.

2 Add the egg and pumpkin and stir until well blended. Sift in the flour, salt, baking soda, cinnamon and nutmeg. Fold just enough to blend; do not overmix.

3 Fold in the currants or raisins. Spoon the batter into the prepared muffin cups, filling them three-quarters full.

4 Bake for 12–15 minutes, until well risen and firm in the middle. Transfer to a rack. Serve warm or cool.

Makes 14

8 tablespoons (1 stick) butter or margarine, at room temperature
⅔ cup dark brown sugar, firmly packed
⅔ cup molasses
1 egg, at room temperature, beaten
8 ounces (1 cup) cooked or canned pumpkin
1¾ cups all-purpose flour
¼ teaspoon salt
1 teaspoon baking soda
1½ teaspoons ground cinnamon
1 teaspoon grated nutmeg
1 ounce (¼ cup) currants or raisins

NUTRITION NOTES

Per portion

Calories	196
Fat	7.3g
Saturated Fat	1.4g
Cholesterol	14mg
Fiber	0.8g

Raisin Bran Muffins

High in fiber and high in flavor, a real treat.

Makes 15

4 tablespoons butter or margarine
¾ cup all-purpose flour
½ cup whole-wheat flour
1½ teaspoons baking soda
⅛ teaspoon salt
1 teaspoon ground cinnamon
½ cup bran
3 ounces (½ cup) raisins
⅓ cup dark brown sugar, firmly packed
¼ cup granulated sugar
1 egg
1 cup buttermilk
juice of ½ lemon

NUTRITION NOTES

Per portion	
Calories	131
Fat	4.1g
Saturated Fat	0.9g
Cholesterol	13mg
Fiber	1.7g

1 Preheat the oven to 400°F. Grease 15 muffin cups or use paper liners.

2 Place the butter or margarine in a heavy saucepan and melt over gentle heat.

3 In a mixing bowl, sift together the all-purpose flour, whole-wheat flour, baking soda, salt and cinnamon.

4 Add the bran, raisins and sugars and stir until blended.

5 In another bowl, mix together the egg, buttermilk, lemon juice and melted butter.

6 Add the buttermilk mixture to the dry ingredients. Stir lightly and quickly just until moistened; do not mix until smooth, as this will ruin the texture.

7 Spoon the batter into the prepared muffin cups, filling them almost to the top. Half-fill any empty cups with water before placing in the oven.

8 Bake until golden, 15–20 minutes. Serve at room temperature.

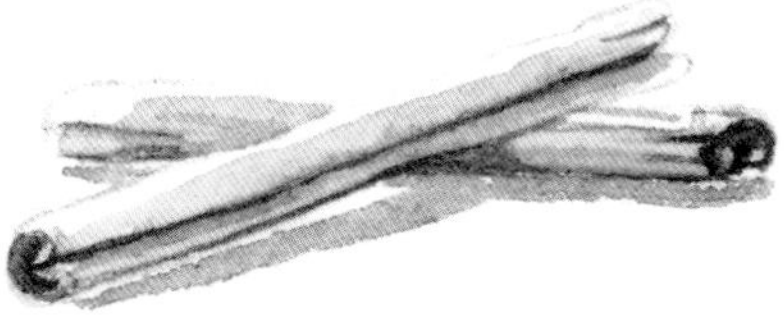

Prune Muffins

All sorts of fruit can be used to make a delicious filling for muffins—prunes are a healthy alternative.

Makes 12
1 egg
1 cup skim milk
¼ cup vegetable oil
¼ cup granulated sugar
2 tablespoons dark brown sugar
2 cups all-purpose flour
2 teaspoons baking powder
½ teaspoon salt
¼ teaspoon grated nutmeg
¾ cup cooked pitted
prunes, chopped

NUTRITION NOTES

Per portion

Calories	177
Fat	4.6g
Saturated Fat	0.6g
Cholesterol	16mg
Fiber	1.5g

1 Preheat the oven to 400°F. Grease a 12-cup muffin pan or use paper liners.

2 Break the egg into a mixing bowl and beat with a fork. Beat in the milk and oil. Stir in the sugars. Set aside.

3 Sift the flour, baking powder, salt and nutmeg into a mixing bowl. Make a well in the center, pour in the egg mixture and stir until moistened. Do not overmix; the batter should be slightly lumpy.

4 Fold in the prunes.

5 Fill the prepared cups two-thirds full. Bake until golden brown, about 20 minutes. Let stand for 10 minutes before unmolding. Serve warm or at room temperature.

Yogurt Honey Muffins

Serve with plain low-fat yogurt and a drizzle of honey for a delicious treat.

1 Preheat the oven to 375°F. Grease a 12-cup muffin pan or use paper liners.

2 In a saucepan, melt the butter and honey. Remove from the heat and set aside to cool slightly.

3 In a bowl, beat together the yogurt, egg, lemon rind and juice.

4 In another bowl, sift together the dry ingredients.

5 Fold the dry ingredients into the yogurt mixture just to blend.

6 Fill the prepared cups two-thirds full. Bake for 20–25 minutes, until well risen and firm in the middle. Let cool in the pan for 5 minutes before unmolding. Serve warm or at room temperature.

Makes 12

4 tablespoons butter
5 tablespoons honey
8 ounces (1 cup) plain yogurt
1 large egg, at room temperature
grated rind of 1 lemon
¼ cup fresh lemon juice
1 cup all-purpose flour
1 cup whole-wheat flour
1½ teaspoons baking soda
⅛ teaspoon grated nutmeg

NUTRITION NOTES

Per portion

Calories	131
Fat	4.1g
Saturated Fat	1.2g
Cholesterol	13mg
Fiber	1.7g

Variation

For Walnut Yogurt Honey Muffins, add 2 ounces (½ cup) chopped walnuts, folding in with the flour. This makes a more substantial muffin.

Blackberry, Liqueur and Rose Water Muffins

Bring a taste of the countryside to teatime with tantalizing wild berries and delicate rose water.

Makes 12

2½ cups all-purpose flour
generous ¼ cup light
brown sugar
4 teaspoons baking powder
pinch of salt
2¼ ounces (generous 1 cup) chopped
blanched almonds
3½ ounces (generous ½ cup)
fresh blackberries
2 eggs
1 cup milk
4 tablespoons melted butter
1 tablespoon fruit liqueur
1 tablespoon rose water

NUTRITION NOTES

Per portion
Calories	194
Fat	8.1g
Saturated Fat	1.32g
Cholesterol	32.8mg
Fiber	1.4g

1 Preheat the oven to 400°F. Grease a 12-cup muffin pan or use paper liners. Mix the flour, sugar, baking powder and salt in a bowl and stir in the almonds and blackberries, mixing them well to coat with the flour mixture.

2 In another bowl, mix the eggs with the milk, then gradually add the butter, fruit liqueur and rose water. Make a well in the center of the dry ingredients and add the egg and milk mixture. Stir well.

3 Spoon the mixture into the greased muffin pan or liners. Bake for 20–25 minutes, or until browned. Turn out the muffins onto a wire rack to cool. Serve with butter.

Date and Apple Muffins

You will only need one or two of these wholesome muffins per person; they are very filling.

1 Preheat the oven to 400°F. Grease a 12-cup muffin pan or use paper liners. Put the whole-wheat flour in a mixing bowl. Sift in the white flour with the cinnamon, baking powder and salt. Rub in the margarine until the mixture resembles bread crumbs, then stir in the brown sugar.

2 Quarter and core the apple, chop the flesh finely and set aside. Stir a little of the apple juice with the pear and apple spread until smooth. Mix in the remaining juice, then add to the flour mixture with the egg. Add the chopped apple to the bowl with the dates. Mix quickly until just combined.

3 Divide the mixture evenly among the muffin cups.

4 Sprinkle with the chopped pecans. Bake the muffins for 20–25 minutes, until golden brown and firm in the middle. Transfer to a wire rack and serve while still warm.

Cook's Tip
Use a pear in place of the apple and chopped dried apricots or other dried fruit in place of the dates. Apple pie spice is a good alternative to cinnamon.

Makes 12

1¼ cups whole-wheat flour
1¼ cups self-rising white flour
1 teaspoon ground cinnamon
2½ teaspoons baking powder
⅛ teaspoon salt
2 tablespoons soft margarine
½ cup light brown sugar
1 eating apple
1 cup apple juice
2 tablespoons pear and apple or other fruit spread
1 egg, lightly beaten
3 ounces (½ cup) chopped dates
1 tablespoon chopped pecans

NUTRITION NOTES
Per portion
Calories	163
Fat	2.98g
Saturated Fat	0.47g
Cholesterol	16.04mg
Fiber	1.97g

Cherry-Marmalade Muffins

Serve with marmalade for a tasty breakfast.

Makes 12

2 cups self-rising flour
1 teaspoon apple pie spice
6 tablespoons sugar
4 ounces (½ cup) candied
cherries, quartered
2 tablespoons orange marmalade
½ cup skim milk
4 tablespoons soft sunflower
margarine
marmalade, to brush

NUTRITION NOTES

Per portion
Calories	154
Fat	3.66g
Saturated Fat	0.68g
Cholesterol	0.54mg
Fiber	0.69g

1 Preheat the oven to 400°F. Lightly grease a 12-cup muffin pan or use paper liners.

2 Sift together the flour and spice, then stir in the sugar and cherries.

3 Mix the marmalade with the milk and beat into the dry ingredients with the margarine. Spoon into the greased pans. Bake for 20–25 minutes, until golden brown and firm in the middle.

4 Turn out onto a wire rack and brush the tops with warmed marmalade. Serve warm or at room temperature.

Fruit Salad Slices

Try this delicious alternative to a traditional fruit cake.

1 Soak the dried fruits in the tea for several hours, or overnight. Drain and reserve the liquid.

2 Preheat the oven to 350°F. Grease a 7-inch round cake pan and line the bottom with baking parchment.

4 Spoon the mixture into the prepared pan and sprinkle with raw sugar. Bake for 50–55 minutes, or until firm. Turn out and cool on a wire rack.

Serves 8

6 ounces (¼ cup) roughly chopped dried fruit mixture, e.g. apples, apricots, prunes and peaches
1 cup hot black tea
2 cups whole-wheat flour
3 teaspoons baking powder
¼ teaspoon salt
1 teaspoon grated nutmeg
4 tablespoons dark brown sugar
3 tablespoons sunflower oil
3 tablespoons skim milk
raw sugar, to sprinkle

NUTRITION NOTES

Per portion

Calories	201
Fat	4.99g
Saturated Fat	0.65g
Cholesterol	0.1mg
Fiber	3.89g

3 Sift the flour into a bowl with the baking powder, salt and nutmeg. Stir in the brown sugar, fruit and tea. Add the oil and milk and mix well.

Pineapple and Cinnamon Drop Scones

Making the batter with pineapple juice instead of milk cuts down on fat and adds to the taste.

Makes 24

1 cup whole-wheat flour
1 cup self-rising white flour
1½ teaspoons baking powder
⅛ teaspoon salt
1 teaspoon ground cinnamon
1 tablespoon sugar
1 egg
1¼ cups pineapple juice
3 ounces (½ cup) dried pineapple, chopped

NUTRITION NOTES

Per portion
Calories	15
Fat	0.81g
Saturated Fat	0.14g
Cholesterol	8.02mg
Fiber	0.76g

1 Preheat a griddle, heavy frying pan or electric frying pan. Put the whole-wheat flour in a mixing bowl. Sift in the white flour, baking powder and salt, add the cinnamon and sugar and make a well.

2 Add the egg with half the pineapple juice and gradually incorporate the surrounding flour to make a smooth batter. Beat in the remaining juice with the chopped pineapple.

3 Lightly grease the griddle or pan. Drop tablespoons of the batter onto the surface, leaving them until they bubble and the bubbles begin to burst.

4 Turn the drop scones with a spatula and cook until the underside is golden brown. Keep the cooked scones warm and moist by wrapping them in a clean napkin while continuing to cook successive batches.

Drop Scones

These little scones are delicious spread with jam.

1 Preheat a griddle, heavy frying pan or electric frying pan. Sift the flour and salt into a mixing bowl. Stir in the sugar and make a well in the center.

2 Add the egg and half the milk, then gradually incorporate the surrounding flour to make a smooth batter. Beat in the remaining milk.

3 Lightly oil the griddle or pan. Drop tablespoons of the batter onto the surface, leaving them until they bubble and the bubbles begin to burst.

4 Turn the drop scones over with a spatula and cook until the underside is golden brown. Keep the cooked drop scones warm and moist by wrapping them in a clean napkin while cooking successive batches.

Makes 18
2 cups self-rising flour
½ teaspoon salt
1 tablespoon sugar
1 egg, beaten
1¼ cups skim milk
oil, for frying

NUTRITION NOTES
Per portion

Calories	64
Fat	1.09g
Saturated Fat	0.2g
Cholesterol	11.04mg
Fiber	0.43g

Cook's Tip
For savory scones, omit the sugar and add 2 chopped scallions and 1 tablespoon freshly grated Parmesan cheese. Serve with cottage cheese.

Whole-Wheat Scones

Made with a mixture of flours, these scones are a healthy high-fiber alternative.

Makes 16

12 tablespoons (1½ sticks) cold butter
2 cups whole-wheat flour
1 cup all-purpose flour
2 tablespoons sugar
½ teaspoon salt
2½ teaspoons baking soda
2 eggs
¾ cup buttermilk
1 ounce (¼ cup) raisins

NUTRITION NOTES

Per portion
Calories	197
Fat	9.8g
Saturated Fat	2g
Cholesterol	25mg
Fiber	2g

1 Preheat the oven to 400°F. Grease and flour a large baking sheet.

2 Cut the butter into small pieces with a blunt knife.

3 Combine the dry ingredients in a bowl. Add the butter and cut in with a pastry blender until the mixture resembles coarse crumbs. Set aside.

4 In another bowl, beat together the eggs and buttermilk. Set aside 2 tablespoons of the mixture for glazing.

5 Stir the remaining egg mixture into the dry ingredients until dough just holds together. Stir in the raisins.

6 Roll out the dough about ¾ inch thick. Stamp out rounds with a cutter. Place on the prepared sheet and brush with the reserved glaze.

7 Bake for 12–15 minutes, until golden. Allow to cool slightly before serving.

Orange Raisin Scones

A tang of orange gives these scones a special flavor.

1 Preheat the oven to 425°F. Grease and flour a large baking sheet.

2 Combine the dry ingredients in a large bowl. Add the butter and margarine and cut in with a pastry blender until the mixture resembles coarse crumbs.

3 Add the orange rind and raisins. Gradually stir in the buttermilk to form a soft dough.

4 Roll out the dough about ¾ inch thick. Stamp out rounds with a cutter.

5 Place on the prepared sheet and brush the tops with milk. Bake for 12–15 minutes, until golden. Serve hot or warm.

Makes 16

2 cups all-purpose flour
1½ tablespoons baking powder
⅓ cup sugar
½ teaspoon salt
5 tablespoons butter, diced
5 tablespoons margarine, diced
grated rind of 1 large orange
2 ounces (⅓ cup) raisins
½ cup buttermilk
milk, for glazing

NUTRITION NOTES

Per portion

Calories	164
Fat	7.9g
Saturated Fat	1.6g
Cholesterol	1mg
Fiber	0.7g

Cook's Tip

For light, tender scones, handle the dough as little as possible. If you wish, split the scones when cool and toast them under a preheated broiler. Butter while still hot.

Sunflower Golden Raisin Scones

Add a bit of crunch to your scones with this combination of sunflower seeds and golden raisins.

Makes 10–12
2 cups self-rising flour
1 teaspoon baking powder
2 tablespoons soft sunflower margarine
2 tablespoons raw sugar
2 ounces (⅓ cup) golden raisins
2 tablespoons sunflower seeds
5 ounces (⅔ cup) plain yogurt
2–3 tablespoons skim milk

NUTRITION NOTES
Per portion

Calories	176
Fat	5.32g
Saturated Fat	0.81g
Cholesterol	0.84mg
Fiber	1.26g

1 Preheat the oven to 450°F. Lightly oil a baking sheet. Sift the flour and baking powder into a bowl and rub in the margarine evenly.

2 Stir in the sugar, golden raisins and half the sunflower seeds, then mix in the yogurt, with just enough milk to make a fairly soft, but not sticky, dough.

3 Roll out on a lightly floured surface to about ¾ inch thick. Cut into 2½-inch flower shapes or rounds with a cookie cutter and lift onto the baking sheet.

4 Brush with milk and sprinkle with the reserved sunflower seeds, then bake for 10–12 minutes, until well risen and golden brown.

5 Cool the scones on a wire rack. Serve split and spread with jam or low-fat spread.

Prune and Citrus Peel Rock Buns

Split these buns and serve with fromage frais, if desired.

1 Preheat the oven to 400°F. Lightly oil a large baking sheet. Sift together the flour and baking powder, then stir in the sugar, prunes, peel and lemon rind.

2 Mix the oil and milk, then stir into the mixture, to make a dough that just binds together.

3 Spoon into rocky heaps on the baking sheet and bake for 20 minutes, until golden. Cool on a wire rack.

Makes 12

2 cups all-purpose flour
2 teaspoons baking powder
⅔ cup raw sugar
2 ounces (½ cup) chopped prunes
2 ounces (⅓ cup) chopped mixed peel
finely grated rind of 1 lemon
¼ cup sunflower oil
5 tablespoons skim milk

NUTRITION NOTES
Per portion

Calories	135
Fat	3.35g
Saturated Fat	0.44g
Cholesterol	0.13mg
Fiber	0.86g

Banana and Apricot Chelsea Buns

These buns are old favorites given a low-fat twist with a delectable fruit filling.

Serves 9

6 tablespoons warm skim milk
1 teaspoon active dry yeast
pinch of sugar
2 cups bread flour
2 teaspoons apple pie spice
½ teaspoon salt
¼ cup granulated sugar
2 tablespoons soft margarine
1 egg

For the filling

1 large ripe banana
6 ounces (1 cup) dried apricots
2 tablespoons granulated sugar
2 tablespoons light brown sugar

For the glaze

2 tablespoons granulated sugar
2 tablespoons water

Cook's Tip

Do not leave the buns in the pans for too long, or the glaze will stick to the sides, making them very difficult to remove.

NUTRITION NOTES

Per portion

Calories	214
Fat	2.18g
Saturated Fat	0.63g
Cholesterol	21.59mg
Fiber	2.18g

1 Lightly grease a 7-inch square pan. Put the warm milk in a jug and sprinkle the yeast on top. Add a pinch of sugar to help activate the yeast, mix well and let sit for 30 minutes.

2 Sift the flour, spice and salt into a mixing bowl. Stir in the granulated sugar, rub in the margarine, then add the yeast mixture and the egg. Gradually mix in the flour to make a soft dough, adding extra milk if needed.

3 Turn out the dough onto a floured surface and knead for 5 minutes, until smooth and elastic. Return the dough to the clean bowl, cover with a damp dish towel and let sit in a warm place for about 2 hours, until doubled in bulk.

4 To prepare the filling, mash the banana in a bowl. Using scissors, snip the apricots into pieces, then stir into the banana with the sugars.

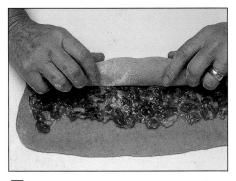

5 Knead the dough on a floured surface for 2 minutes, then roll out to a 12 x 9-inch rectangle. Spread the banana and apricot filling over the dough and roll up lengthwise like a jelly roll, with the seam underneath.

6 Cut the roll into 9 buns. Place, cut side down, in the pan, cover and allow to rise for 30 minutes. Preheat the oven to 400°F and bake for 20–25 minutes. Meanwhile, mix the granulated sugar and water in a small saucepan. Heat, stirring, until dissolved, then boil for 2 minutes. Brush the glaze over the baked buns while still hot.

Blueberry Streusel Slice

This soft berry filling tastes delicious with the nutty topping.

Makes about 30 slices

8 ounces ready-made shortcrust pastry
½ cup all-purpose flour
¼ teaspoon baking powder
3 tablespoons butter or margarine
⅓ cup light brown sugar
2 tablespoons fresh white bread crumbs
¼ teaspoon salt
4 tablespoons sliced or
chopped almonds
4 tablespoons blackberry jelly
4 ounces blueberries, fresh or frozen

NUTRITION NOTES

Per portion
Calories	77
Fat	4.16g
Saturated Fat	1.57g
Cholesterol	5.84mg
Fiber	0.95g

1 Preheat the oven to 350°F. Roll out the pastry on a lightly floured surface to line a 7 x 11-inch jelly roll pan. Prick the bottom evenly with a fork.

2 Rub together the flour, baking powder, butter or margarine, sugar, bread crumbs and salt until crumbly, then mix in the almonds.

3 Spread the pastry with the jelly, sprinkle with the blueberries, then cover evenly with the streusel topping, pressing down lightly. Bake for 20 minutes, then reduce the temperature to 325°F and cook for another 10–20 minutes.

4 Remove from the oven when golden on the top and the pastry is cooked through. Cut into slices while still hot, then allow to cool.

Sticky Date and Apple Bars

If possible, allow these to mature for a day or two before cutting—they will get stickier and better!

Makes about 16 bars

8 tablespoons (1 stick) margarine
4 tablespoons dark brown sugar
4 tablespoons golden syrup
4 ounces (¾ cup) chopped dates
1¼ cups rolled oats
1 cup whole-wheat flour
1½ teaspoons baking powder
⅛ teaspoon salt
2 eating apples (about 8 ounces),
peeled, cored and grated
1–2 teaspoons lemon juice
20–25 walnut halves

1 Preheat the oven to 375°F. Line a 7–8-inch square or rectangular bottomed cake pan. In a large pan, heat the margarine, sugar, syrup and dates, stirring until the dates soften completely.

2 Mix in the oats, flour, baking powder, salt, apples and lemon juice. Spoon into the pan and spread out evenly. Top with the walnut halves.

3 Bake for 30 minutes, then reduce the temperature to 325°F and bake for 10–20 minutes more, until golden and firm to the touch. Cut into squares or bars while still warm, and keep for 1–2 days before eating.

NUTRITION NOTES

Per portion

Calories	183
Fat	10.11g
Saturated Fat	1.64g
Cholesterol	0.14mg
Fiber	1g

Apricot Sponge Bars

These bars are delicious with tea—the apricots keep them moist for several days.

Makes 18

2 cups self-rising flour
½ cup light brown sugar
½ cup semolina
1 cup dried apricots, chopped
2 tablespoons honey
2 tablespoons malt extract
2 eggs
4 tablespoons skim milk
4 tablespoons sunflower oil
a few drops of almond extract
2 tablespoons sliced almonds

NUTRITION NOTES

Per portion
Calories	153
Fat	4.5g
Saturated Fat	0.61g
Cholesterol	21.5mg
Fiber	1.27g

1 Preheat the oven to 325°F. Lightly grease and then line a 7 x 11-inch baking pan.

2 Sift the flour into a bowl and mix in the sugar, semolina and apricots. Make a well in the center and add the honey, malt extract, eggs, milk, oil and almond extract. Mix the ingredients together thoroughly until smooth.

3 Spoon the mixture into the pan, spreading it to the edges, then sprinkle the sliced almonds on top.

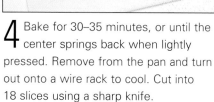

4 Bake for 30–35 minutes, or until the center springs back when lightly pressed. Remove from the pan and turn out onto a wire rack to cool. Cut into 18 slices using a sharp knife.

Cook's Tip

If you can't find pre-soaked apricots, use chopped ordinary dried apricots soaked in boiling water for 1 hour, then drain and add to the mixture.

Apricot Yogurt Cookies

These soft cookies are very quick to make and are useful for packed lunches.

1 Preheat the oven to 375°F. Lightly oil a large baking sheet.

2 Sift together the flour, baking powder and cinnamon. Stir in the oats, sugar, apricots and nuts.

3 Beat together the yogurt and oil, then stir evenly into the mixture to make a firm dough. If necessary, add a little more yogurt.

4 Use your hands to roll the mixture into about 16 small balls, place on the baking sheet and flatten with a fork.

5 Sprinkle with raw sugar. Bake for 15–20 minutes, or until firm and golden brown. Transfer to a wire rack and let cool.

Makes 16

1½ cups all-purpose flour
1 teaspoon baking powder
1 teaspoon ground cinnamon
1 cup rolled oats
½ cup light brown sugar
4 ounces (½ cup) chopped
dried apricots
1 tablespoon sliced hazelnuts or
almonds
5 ounces (⅔ cup) plain yogurt
3 tablespoons sunflower oil
raw sugar, to sprinkle

NUTRITION NOTES
Per portion
Calories   95
Fat   2.66g
Saturated Fat   0.37g
Cholesterol   0.3mg
Fiber   0.94g

Cook's Tip
These cookies do not keep well, so it is best to eat them within two days or to freeze them. Pack in plastic bags and freeze for up to four months.

Buttermilk Biscuits

Low in fat, these biscuits are perfect for a midmorning snack.

Makes 15

1½ cups all-purpose flour

1 teaspoon salt

1 teaspoon baking powder

2½ teaspoons baking soda

4 tablespoons cold butter or margarine

¾ cup buttermilk

NUTRITION NOTES

Per portion

Calories	85
Fat	3.5g
Saturated Fat	0.7g
Cholesterol	0.5mg
Fiber	0.5g

1 Preheat the oven to 425°F. Grease a baking sheet. Sift the dry ingredients into a bowl. Cut in the butter or margarine with a pastry blender until the mixture resembles coarse crumbs.

2 Gradually pour in the buttermilk, stirring with a fork to form a soft dough.

3 Roll out the biscuit dough to about ½ inch thick.

4 Stamp out 2-inch rounds with a biscuit cutter. Place on the prepared baking sheet and bake for 12–15 minutes, or until golden. Serve warm or at room temperature.

Shortcake

Delicious served warm with a low-fat spread.

1 Preheat the oven to 425°F. Grease a baking sheet.

2 Sift the flour, sugar, baking powder and salt into a bowl.

3 Cut in the butter with a pastry blender until the mixture resembles coarse crumbs.

4 Pour in the milk and stir with a fork to form a soft dough.

5 Roll out the dough to about ¼ inch thick. Stamp out rounds with a 2½-inch biscuit cutter. Place on the prepared sheet and bake for about 12 minutes, or until golden. Serve hot or warm.

Makes 8

1⅓ cups all-purpose flour
2 tablespoons sugar
3 teaspoons baking powder
⅛ teaspoon salt
5 tablespoons cold butter, cut in pieces
½ cup skim milk

NUTRITION NOTES

Per portion

Calories	176
Fat	8g
Saturated Fat	1.5g
Cholesterol	1mg
Fiber	0.8g

Variation

For Berry Shortcake, split the cakes in half while still warm. Top one half with lightly sugared fresh berries such as strawberries, raspberries or blueberries, and sandwich with the other half. Serve with dollops of thick low-fat yogurt.

Oaty Crisps

These cookies are very crisp and crunchy—ideal to serve with morning coffee.

Makes 18
1¾ cups rolled oats
½ cup light brown sugar
1 egg
4 tablespoons sunflower oil
2 tablespoons malt extract

NUTRITION NOTES
Per portion

Calories	86
Fat	3.59g
Saturated Fat	0.57g
Cholesterol	10.7mg
Fiber	0.66g

1 Preheat the oven to 375°F. Lightly grease two baking sheets. Mix the rolled oats and sugar in a bowl, breaking up any lumps in the sugar. Add the egg, sunflower oil and malt extract, mix well, then allow to soak for 15 minutes.

2 Using a teaspoon, place small heaps of the mixture well apart on the prepared baking sheets. Press the heaps into 3-inch rounds with the back of a dampened fork.

3 Bake the cookies for 10–15 minutes, until golden brown. Allow them to cool for 1 minute, then remove with a spatula and cool on a wire rack.

Cook's Tip
To give these cookies a coarser texture, substitute jumbo oats for some or all of the rolled oats. Once cool, store them in an airtight container to keep them as crisp and fresh as possible.

Orange Cookies

A popular choice for a well-earned coffee break.

1 With an electric mixer, cream the butter and sugar until light and fluffy. Add the yolks, orange juice and rind, and continue beating to blend. Set aside.

2 In another bowl, sift together the flours, salt and baking powder. Add this to the butter mixture and stir until it forms a dough.

3 Wrap the dough in waxed paper and chill for 2 hours.

4 Preheat the oven to 375°F. Grease two baking sheets.

5 Roll spoonfuls of the dough into balls and place 1–2 inches apart on the prepared sheets.

6 Press down with a fork to flatten. Bake for 8–10 minutes, until golden brown. With a metal spatula, transfer to a rack to cool.

Makes 30

8 tablespoons (1 stick) butter, at room temperature
1 cup sugar
2 egg yolks
1 tablespoon fresh orange juice
grated rind of 1 orange
1 cup all-purpose flour
½ cup cake flour
½ teaspoon salt
1 teaspoon baking powder

NUTRITION NOTES
Per portion

Calories	84
Fat	3.5g
Saturated Fat	0.7g
Cholesterol	14mg
Fiber	0.2g

Breads

The aroma of freshly
baked bread makes
every house feel like
home. And these low-fat
loaves also taste
tantalizingly good.

White Bread

The classic white loaf, perfect for breakfast toast.

Makes 2 loaves
¼ cup lukewarm water
2 teaspoons active dry yeast
2 tablespoons sugar
2 cups lukewarm skim milk
2 tablespoons butter or margarine, at room temperature
2 teaspoons salt
6–6½ cups all-purpose flour

NUTRITION NOTES

Per portion

Calories	178
Fat	1.8g
Saturated Fat	0.3g
Cholesterol	0.6g
Fiber	1.4g

1 Combine the water, yeast and 1 tablespoon of sugar in a measuring cup and let sit for 15 minutes.

2 Pour the milk into a large bowl. Add the remaining sugar, the butter or margarine, the salt and the yeast mixture.

3 Stir in the flour, 1 cup at a time, until a stiff dough is obtained. Alternatively, use a food processor.

4 Transfer the dough to a floured surface. To knead, push the dough away from you with the palm of your hand, then fold it toward you, and push it away again. Repeat until the dough is smooth and elastic.

5 Place the dough in a large greased bowl, cover with a plastic bag, and set aside to rise in a warm place until doubled in volume, 2–3 hours. Grease two 9 x 5-inch loaf pans.

6 Punch down the risen dough with your fist and divide in half. Form into loaf shapes and place in the pans, seam side down. Cover and let rise in a warm place until almost doubled in volume, about 45 minutes.

7 Preheat the oven to 375°F. Bake for 45–50 minutes, until firm and brown. Unmold and tap the bottom of a loaf: If it sounds hollow, the loaf is done. If necessary, return to the oven and bake a few minutes more. Transfer to a rack to cool.

Country Bread

A whole-wheat loaf that is high in fiber and low in fat.

1 For the starter, combine the yeast, water, flour and sugar in a bowl and stir with a fork. Cover and set aside in a warm place for 2–3 hours, or let sit overnight in a cool place.

2 For the bread, place the flours, salt and butter in a food processor and process just until blended, for 1–2 minutes. Stir together the milk and starter, then slowly pour into the processor, with the motor running, until the mixture forms a dough. If necessary, add more water. Alternatively, the dough can be mixed by hand. Transfer to a floured surface and knead until smooth and elastic.

3 Place in an ungreased bowl, cover with a plastic bag, and let rise in a warm place until doubled in volume, about 1½ hours. Transfer to a floured surface and knead briefly. Return to the bowl and let rise until tripled in volume, about 1½ hours.

4 Divide the dough in half. Cut off one-third of the dough from each half and shape into balls. Shape the larger remaining halves into balls. Grease a baking sheet.

5 For each loaf, top the large ball with the small ball and press the center with the handle of a wooden spoon to secure. Slash the top, cover with a plastic bag, and allow to rise.

6 Preheat the oven to 400°F. Dust the dough with whole-wheat flour and bake for 45–50 minutes, until the top is browned and the bottom sounds hollow when tapped. Cool on a wire rack before serving.

Serves 12

2½ cups whole-wheat flour
2½ cups all-purpose flour
1 cup white bread flour
4 teaspoons salt
4 tablespoons butter, at room temperature
2 cups lukewarm skim milk

For the starter

2 teaspoons active dry yeast
1 cup lukewarm water
1 cup all-purpose flour
¼ teaspoon sugar

NUTRITION NOTES

Per portion

Calories	204
Fat	3.3g
Saturated Fat	0.6g
Cholesterol	1mg
Fiber	2.7g

Poppy Seed Rolls

Pile these soft rolls in a basket and serve them for breakfast or with dinner.

Makes 12
1¼ cups warm skim milk
1 teaspoon active dry yeast
pinch of sugar
4 cups bread flour
1 teaspoon salt
1 egg, lightly beaten

For the topping
1 egg, beaten
poppy seeds

Cook's Tip
Use rapid-rise yeast if you prefer.
Add it directly to the dry ingredients and mix with lukewarm milk.
The rolls will only require one rising (see package instructions).
Vary the toppings as you like.
Sesame seeds, sunflower seeds and caraway seeds are all good; try adding caraway seeds to the dough, too, for extra flavor.

NUTRITION NOTES
Per portion

Calories	160
Fat	2.42g
Saturated Fat	0.46g
Cholesterol	32.58mg
Fiber	1.16g

1 Put half the warm milk in a small bowl. Sprinkle the yeast on top. Add the sugar, mix well and let stand for 30 minutes.

2 Sift the flour and salt into a mixing bowl. Make a well in the center and pour in the yeast mixture and the egg. Gradually incorporate the flour, adding enough of the remaining milk to mix to a soft dough.

3 Turn out the dough onto a floured surface and knead for 5 minutes, until smooth and elastic. Return to the clean bowl, cover with a damp dish towel and set aside in a warm place to rise for about 1 hour, until doubled in bulk.

4 Lightly grease two baking sheets. Turn out the dough onto a floured surface. Knead for 2 minutes, then cut into 12 pieces and shape into rolls.

5 Place the rolls on the prepared baking sheets, cover loosely with a large plastic bag (ballooning it to trap the air inside) and let stand in a warm place until the rolls have risen well. Preheat the oven to 425°.

6 Glaze the rolls with the beaten egg, sprinkle with poppy seeds and bake for 12–15 minutes, until golden brown. Transfer to a wire rack to cool.

Braided Loaf

An attractive, traditional loaf that would be fun as a dinner party accompaniment.

Serves 10

2 teaspoons active dry yeast
1 teaspoon honey
1 cup lukewarm skim milk
4 tablespoons butter, melted
3 cups all-purpose flour
1 teaspoon salt
1 egg, lightly beaten
1 egg yolk, beaten with 1 teaspoon skim milk, for glazing

NUTRITION NOTES

Per portion

Calories	222
Fat	6.6g
Saturated Fat	1.35g
Cholesterol	40.3mg
Fiber	1.4g

1 Combine the yeast, honey, milk and butter, stir, and let sit for 15 minutes to dissolve.

2 In a large bowl, mix together the flour and salt. Make a well in the center and add the yeast mixture and egg. With a wooden spoon, stir from the center, incorporating flour with each turn, to obtain a rough dough.

3 Transfer to a floured surface and knead until smooth and elastic. Place in a clean bowl, cover, and let rise in a warm place until doubled in volume, about 1½ hours.

4 Grease a baking sheet. Punch down the dough and divide into three equal pieces. Roll to shape each piece into a long, thin strip.

5 Begin braiding from the center strip, tucking in the ends to conceal them. Cover loosely and let rise in a warm place for 30 minutes.

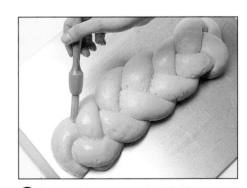

6 Preheat the oven to 375°F. Place the bread in a cool place while the oven heats. Brush with the glaze and bake until golden, 40–45 minutes. Set on a rack to cool completely before serving.

Sesame Seed Bread

Sesame seeds have a distinctive flavor as well as a crunchy texture.

1 Combine the yeast and ¼ cup of the water and let sit to dissolve. Mix the flours and salt in a large bowl. Make a well in the center and pour in the yeast and the remaining water.

2 With a wooden spoon, stir from the center, incorporating flour with each turn, to obtain a rough dough.

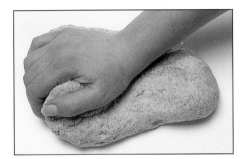

3 Transfer to a floured surface. To knead, push the dough away from you with the palm of your hand, then fold it toward you, and push away again. Repeat until smooth and elastic, then return to the bowl and cover with a plastic bag. Let sit in a warm place until doubled in volume, 1½–2 hours.

4 Grease a 9-inch cake pan. Punch down the dough and knead in the sesame seeds. Divide the dough into 16 balls and place in the pan. Cover with a plastic bag and set aside in a warm place until risen above the rim of the pan.

5 Preheat the oven to 425°F. Brush the top of the loaf with milk and sprinkle with the sesame seeds. Bake for 15 minutes. Lower the heat to 375°F and bake until the bottom of the loaf sounds hollow when tapped, about 30 minutes more. Cool on a rack.

Serves 10–12

2 teaspoons active dry yeast
1½ cups lukewarm water
1½ cups all-purpose flour
1½ cups whole-wheat flour
2 teaspoons salt
½ cup toasted sesame seeds
milk, for glazing
2 tablespoons sesame seeds, for sprinkling

NUTRITION NOTES

Per portion

Calories	218
Fat	7.5g
Saturated Fat	1.1g
Cholesterol	0
Fiber	3.6g

Parker House Rolls

These easy-to-make rolls are perfect if you're cooking for large numbers.

Makes 48 rolls

2 teaspoons active dry yeast
2 cups lukewarm skim milk
8 tablespoons (1 stick) margarine
5 tablespoons sugar
2 teaspoons salt
2 eggs
7–8 cups all-purpose flour
4 tablespoons butter

NUTRITION NOTES

Per portion

Calories	114
Fat	3.5g
Saturated Fat	0.68g
Cholesterol	8.5mg
Fiber	0.7g

1 Combine the yeast and ½ cup milk in a large bowl. Stir and let sit for 15 minutes to dissolve. Bring the remaining milk to a simmer, cool for 5 minutes, then beat in the margarine, sugar, salt and eggs. Allow to cool to lukewarm.

2 Pour the milk mixture into the yeast mixture. Stir in 4 cups of flour with a wooden spoon. Add the remaining flour, 1 cup at a time, until a rough dough is obtained.

3 Transfer the dough to a lightly floured surface and knead until it is smooth and elastic. Place in a clean bowl, cover with a plastic bag, and set aside to rise in a warm place until doubled in volume, about 2 hours.

4 In a saucepan, melt the butter and set aside. Grease two baking sheets. Punch down the dough and divide into four equal pieces. Roll each piece into an 8 x 12-inch rectangle about ¼ inch thick.

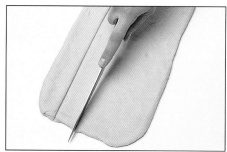

5 Cut each of the rolled-out rectangular pieces into four 2 x 12-inch strips. Cut each strip into three 4 x 2-inch rectangles.

6 Brush each rectangle with melted butter, then fold the rectangles in half, so that the bottom extends about ½ inch beyond the top.

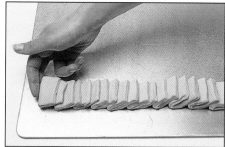

7 Place the rolls slightly overlapping on the baking sheet, with the shorter side facing up.

8 Cover and chill for 30 minutes. Preheat the oven to 350°F. Bake until golden, 18–20 minutes. Cool the rolls slightly before serving.

Cloverleaf Rolls

Create these pretty rolls by baking them in a muffin pan.

1 Heat the milk until lukewarm; test the temperature with your knuckle. Pour into a large bowl and stir in the sugar, butter and yeast. Let sit for 15 minutes.

2 Stir the egg and salt into the yeast mixture. Gradually stir in 3⅓ cups of the flour. Add just enough extra flour to obtain a rough dough.

3 Knead on a floured surface until smooth and elastic. Place in a greased bowl, cover, and set in a warm place until doubled in volume, about 1½ hours. Grease two 12-cup muffin pans.

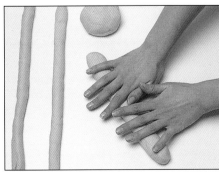

4 Punch down the dough. Cut into four equal pieces. Roll each piece into a rope 14 inches long. Cut each rope into 18 pieces, then roll each into a ball.

5 Place three balls, side by side, in each muffin cup. Cover loosely and let rise in a warm place until doubled in volume, about half an hour.

6 Preheat the oven to 400°F. Brush with glaze. Bake for about 20 minutes, until lightly browned. Cool slightly before serving.

Makes 24
1¼ cups skim milk
2 tablespoons sugar
4 tablespoons butter, at room temperature
2 teaspoons active dry yeast
1 egg
2 teaspoons salt
3½–4 cups flour
melted butter, for glazing

NUTRITION NOTES
Per portion
Calories   109
Fat   2.9g
Saturated Fat   0.6g
Cholesterol   8mg
Fiber   0.7g

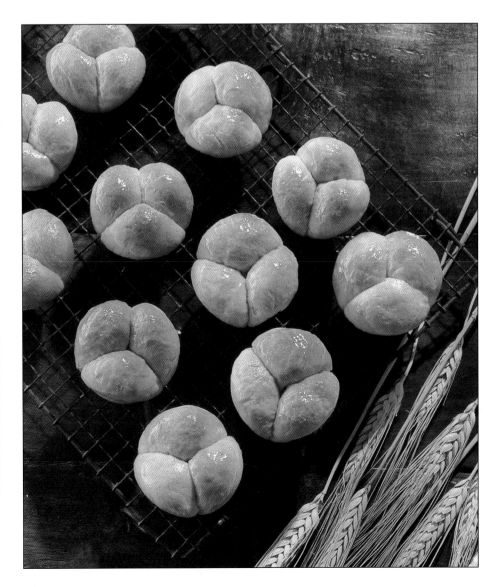

Whole-Wheat Buttermilk Rolls

These traditional whole-wheat rolls are made with buttermilk to keep the fat content low.

Makes 12

2 teaspoons active dry yeast
¼ cup lukewarm water
1 teaspoon sugar
¾ cup lukewarm buttermilk
¼ teaspoon baking soda
1 teaspoon salt
3 tablespoons butter, at room
temperature
1½ cups whole-wheat flour
1 cup all-purpose flour
1 beaten egg, for glazing

NUTRITION NOTES

Per portion

Calories	143
Fat	4.2g
Saturated Fat	0.8g
Cholesterol	17mg
Fiber	2.1g

1 In a large bowl, combine the yeast, water and sugar. Stir, and let sit for 15 minutes to dissolve.

2 Add the buttermilk, baking soda, salt and butter and stir to blend. Stir in the whole-wheat flour.

3 Add just enough of the all-purpose flour to obtain a rough dough. If the dough is stiff, mix it with your hands.

4 Transfer to a floured surface and knead until smooth and elastic. Divide into three equal parts. Roll each into a cylinder, then cut into four pieces.

5 Form the pieces into torpedo shapes. Place on a greased baking sheet, cover, and set aside in a warm place until doubled in volume.

6 Preheat the oven to 400°F. Brush with the glaze. Bake for 15–20 minutes, until firm. Allow to cool.

French Bread

A French stick, or baguette, is perfect for garlic bread or sandwiches.

1 Combine the yeast and water, stir, and let sit for 15 minutes to dissolve. Stir in the salt.

2 Add the flour, 1 cup at a time. Beat in with a wooden spoon, adding just enough flour to obtain a smooth dough. Alternatively, use an electric mixer with a dough hook attachment.

3 Transfer to a floured surface and knead until smooth and elastic.

4 Shape into a ball, place in a greased bowl, and cover with a plastic bag. Set aside to rise in a warm place until doubled in volume, 2–4 hours.

5 Transfer to a lightly floured board, halve the dough and shape into two long loaves. Place on a baking sheet sprinkled with cornmeal, and let rise for 5 minutes.

6 Score the tops in several places with a very sharp knife. Brush with water and place in a cold oven. Set a pan of boiling water on the bottom of the oven and set the oven to 400°F. Bake until crusty and golden, about 40 minutes. Cool on a rack.

Serves 16

2 teaspoons active dry yeast
2 cups lukewarm water
1 teaspoon salt
6–8 cups all-purpose flour
cornmeal, for sprinkling

NUTRITION NOTES

Per portion

Calories	96
Fat	0.37g
Saturated Fat	0.13g
Cholesterol	0
Fiber	0.87g

Buttermilk Graham Bread

If you can't find graham flour, whole-wheat will make an equally delicious loaf.

Serves 8

2 teaspoons active dry yeast
½ cup lukewarm water
2 cups graham or whole-wheat flour
3 cups all-purpose flour
1 cup cornmeal
2 teaspoons salt
2 tablespoons sugar
4 tablespoons butter, at room temperature
2 cups lukewarm buttermilk
1 beaten egg, for glazing
sesame seeds, for sprinkling

NUTRITION NOTES

Per portion
Calories 195
Fat 4g
Saturated Fat 0.8g
Cholesterol 10mg
Fiber 1.9g

1 Combine the yeast and water, stir, and let sit for 15 minutes to dissolve.

2 Mix together the graham or whole-wheat flour, all-purpose flour, cornmeal, salt and sugar in a large bowl. Make a well in the center of the dry ingredients and pour in the yeast mixture, then add the butter and the buttermilk.

3 Stir from the center, mixing in the flour until a rough dough is formed. If too stiff, use your hands.

4 Transfer to a floured surface and knead until smooth. Place in a clean bowl, cover, and let sit in a warm place until doubled, 2–3 hours.

5 Grease two 8-inch square baking pans. Punch down the dough. Divide into eight equal pieces and roll the pieces into balls. Place four balls in each pan. Cover and let sit in a warm place until the dough rises above the rim of the pans, about 1 hour.

6 Preheat the oven to 375°F. Brush with the glaze, then sprinkle the sesame seeds on top. Bake for about 50 minutes, or until the bottoms sound hollow when tapped. Cool on a wire rack.

Multigrain Bread

Try replacing the wheat germ or soy flour with rye, barley or buckwheat.

1 Combine the yeast and water, stir, and let sit for 15 minutes to dissolve.

2 Place the oats in a large bowl. Heat the milk until scalded, then pour it over the oats.

3 Stir in the salt, oil, sugar and honey. Let the mixture cool to 85°F.

4 Stir in the yeast mixture, eggs, wheat germ and soy and whole-wheat flours. Gradually stir in enough all-purpose flour to obtain a rough dough.

5 Transfer the dough to a floured surface and knead, adding flour if necessary, until smooth and elastic. Return to a clean bowl, cover, and let rise in a warm place until doubled in volume, 2–2½ hours.

6 Grease two 8 x 4-inch bread pans. Punch down the risen dough with your fist and knead briefly.

7 Divide the dough into quarters. Roll each quarter into a cylinder 1½ inches thick. Twist together two cylinders and place in a pan; repeat for remaining cylinders.

8 Cover and let rise until doubled in size, about 1 hour.

9 Preheat the oven to 375°F.

10 Bake the loaves for 45–50 minutes in the center of the oven, until the bottoms sound hollow when tapped lightly. Remove from the pans and allow to cool on a rack.

Makes 2 loaves

2 teaspoons active dry yeast
¼ cup lukewarm water
1 cup rolled oats
2 cups skim milk
2 teaspoons salt
¼ cup oil
¼ cup brown sugar, firmly packed
2 tablespoons honey
2 eggs, lightly beaten
½ cup wheat germ
1 cup soy flour
2 cups whole-wheat flour
3–3½ cups all-purpose flour

NUTRITION NOTES

Per portion

Calories	238
Fat	4.4g
Saturated Fat	0.64g
Cholesterol	19.7mg
Fiber	4.2g

Austrian Three-Grain Bread

A mixture of grains gives this dense-textured bread a delightful nutty flavor.
Make two smaller twists, if preferred.

Serves 8–10

2 cups warm water
2 teaspoons active dry yeast
pinch of sugar
2 cups bread flour
1½ teaspoons salt
2 cups wholemeal bread flour
2 cups rye flour
2 tablespoons flax seed
½ cup rolled oats
3 tablespoons sunflower seeds
2 tablespoons malt extract

NUTRITION NOTES

Per portion	
Calories	367
Fat	5.36g
Saturated Fat	0.6g
Cholesterol	0
Fiber	6.67g

1 Put half the water in a jug. Sprinkle the yeast on top. Add the sugar, mix well and let sit for 10 minutes.

2 Sift the white flour and salt into a mixing bowl and add the other flours. Set aside 1 teaspoon of the flax seed and add the rest to the flour mixture with the rolled oats and sunflower seeds. Make a well in the center. Add the yeast mixture to the bowl with the malt extract and the remaining water.

3 Gradually incorporate the flour.

4 Mix to a soft dough, adding extra water if necessary. Turn out onto a floured surface and knead for about 5 minutes, until smooth and elastic. Return to the clean bowl, cover with a damp dish towel and let rise for about 2 hours, until doubled in bulk.

5 Grease a baking sheet. Turn out the dough onto a floured surface, knead for 2 minutes, then divide in half. Roll each half into a 12-inch-long sausage.

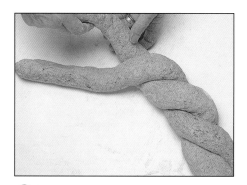

6 Twist the two sausages together, dampen the ends and press to seal. Lift the twist onto the prepared baking sheet. Brush the braid with water, sprinkle with the remaining flax seed and cover loosely with a large plastic bag (ballooning it to trap the air inside). Let sit in a warm place until well risen. Preheat the oven to 425°F.

7 Bake the loaf for 10 minutes, then lower the oven temperature to 400°F and bake for 20 minutes more, or until the loaf sounds hollow when it is tapped on the bottom. Transfer to a wire rack to cool.

Granary Rolls

These make excellent picnic fare, filled with cottage cheese, tuna, salad and low-fat mayonnaise. They are also very good served warm with soup.

Makes 8
1¼ cups warm water
1 teaspoon active dry yeast
pinch of sugar
4 cups malted brown flour
1 teaspoon salt
1 tablespoon malt extract
1 tablespoon rolled oats

Cook's Tip
To make a large loaf, shape the dough into a round, flatten it slightly and bake for 30–40 minutes. Test by tapping the bottom of the loaf—if it sounds hollow, it is done.

NUTRITION NOTES
Per portion

Calories	223
Fat	1.14g
Saturated Fat	0.16g
Cholesterol	0
Fiber	3.1g

1 Put half the warm water in a jug. Sprinkle in the yeast. Add the sugar, mix well and let sit for 10 minutes.

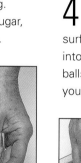

2 Put the malted brown flour and salt in a mixing bowl and make a well in the center. Add the yeast mixture with the malt extract and the remaining water. Gradually incorporate the flour and mix to a soft dough.

3 Turn the dough onto a floured surface and knead for 5 minutes, until smooth and elastic. Return to the clean bowl, cover with a damp dish towel and set aside in a warm place to rise for about 2 hours, until doubled in bulk.

4 Lightly grease two baking sheets. Turn out the dough onto a floured surface, knead for 2 minutes, then divide into eight pieces. Shape the pieces into balls and flatten them with the palm of your hand to make neat 4-inch rounds.

5 Place the rounds on the prepared baking sheets, cover loosely with a large plastic bag (ballooning it to trap the air inside), and let stand in a warm place until the rolls are well risen. Preheat the oven to 425°F.

6 Brush the rolls with water, sprinkle with the oats and bake for 20–25 minutes, or until they sound hollow when tapped on the bottom. Cool on a wire rack, then serve with the low-fat filling of your choice.

Rye Bread

Rye bread is popular in northern Europe and makes excellent open-faced sandwiches.

Serves 16

3 cups whole-wheat flour
2 cups rye flour
1 cup bread flour
1½ teaspoons salt
2 tablespoons caraway seeds
2 cups warm water
2 teaspoons active dry yeast
pinch of sugar
2 tablespoons molasses

Cook's Tip

To make caraway-seed bread rolls, divide each of the two flattened loaves into eight equal portions. Place them on the baking sheet, brush with water and sprinkle with caraway seeds. Vary the topping by using poppy seeds if you like.

NUTRITION NOTES

Per portion
Calories	156
Fat	1.2g
Saturated Fat	0.05g
Cholesterol	0
Fiber	4.53g

1 Put the flours and salt in a bowl. Set aside 1 teaspoon of the caraway seeds and add the rest to the bowl.

2 Put half the water in a bowl. Sprinkle the yeast on top. Add the sugar, mix well and let sit for 10 minutes.

3 Make a well in the flour mixture, then add the yeast mixture with the molasses and the remaining water. Gradually incorporate the flour and mix to a soft dough, adding a little extra water if necessary.

4 Transfer to a floured surface and knead for 5 minutes, until smooth and elastic. Return to the clean bowl, cover and set aside in a warm place for about 2 hours, until doubled in bulk. Grease a baking sheet.

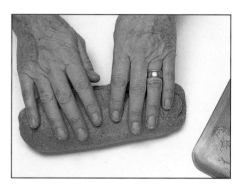

5 Turn out the dough onto a floured surface and knead for 2 minutes. Divide the dough in half, then shape into two 9-inch-long oval loaves. Flatten the loaves slightly and place them on the baking sheet.

6 Brush the loaves with water and sprinkle with the remaining caraway seeds. Cover and set in a warm place for about 40 minutes, until well risen. Preheat the oven to 400°F. Bake the loaves for 30 minutes, or until they sound hollow when tapped on the bottom. Cool on a wire rack. Serve the bread plain, or slice and add a low-fat topping.

Cheese Bread

A tasty bread, perfect for making savory sandwiches.

Serves 10

2 teaspoons active dry yeast
1 cup lukewarm
skim milk
2 tablespoons butter
3 cups all-purpose flour
2 teaspoons salt
1 cup grated sharp Cheddar cheese

NUTRITION NOTES

Per portion

Calories	214
Fat	4.8g
Saturated Fat	1.57g
Cholesterol	5.5mg
Fiber	1.4g

1 Combine the yeast and milk, stir, and let sit for 15 minutes to dissolve. Melt the butter, let cool, and add to the yeast mixture.

2 Mix the flour and salt together in a large bowl. Make a well in the center and pour in the yeast mixture. With a wooden spoon, stir from the center, incorporating flour with each turn, to obtain a rough dough. If the dough seems too dry, add 2–3 tablespoons water.

3 Transfer to a floured surface and knead until smooth and elastic. Return to the bowl, cover and let rise in a warm place until doubled in volume, 2–3 hours.

4 Grease a 9 x 5-inch loaf pan. Punch down the dough with your fist. Knead in the cheese, distributing it as evenly as possible.

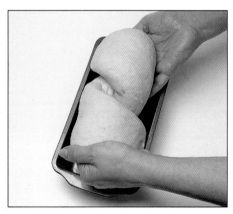

5 Twist the dough, form into a loaf shape and place in the pan, tucking the ends under. Let stand in a warm place until the dough rises above the rim of the pan.

6 Preheat the oven to 400°F. Bake for 15 minutes, then lower the heat to 375°F and bake for about 30 minutes more, until the bottom of the loaf sounds hollow when tapped. Allow to cool on a wire rack.

Anadama Bread

A delicious traditional American yeast bread flavored with molasses.

1 Combine the yeast and lukewarm water, stir well, and let sit for 15 minutes to dissolve.

2 Meanwhile, combine the cornmeal, butter or margarine, molasses and boiling water in a large bowl. Add the yeast, egg, and half the flour. Stir together to blend.

3 Stir in the remaining flour and salt. When the dough becomes too stiff, mix with your hands until it comes away from the sides of the bowl. If it is too sticky, add more flour; if too stiff, add a little water.

4 Knead until smooth and elastic. Place in a bowl, cover with a plastic bag, and set aside in a warm place until doubled in volume, 2–3 hours.

5 Grease two 7 x 3-inch bread pans. Punch down the dough with your fist. Shape into two loaves and place in the pans, seam side down. Cover and set aside in a warm place until risen above the tops of the pans, 1–2 hours.

6 Preheat the oven to 375°F. Bake for 50 minutes. Remove and cool on a rack, or set across the pan to cool.

Makes 2 loaves

1 envelope active dry yeast
4 tablespoons lukewarm water
½ cup cornmeal
3 tablespoons butter or margarine
4 tablespoons molasses
¾ cup boiling water
1 egg
3 cups flour
2 teaspoons salt

NUTRITION NOTES
Per portion
Calories   146
Fat   3.1g
Saturated Fat   1.62g
Cholesterol   18.5mg
Fiber   0.9g

Rosemary and Sea Salt Focaccia

Focaccia is an Italian flatbread made with olive oil. Here it is given added flavor with rosemary and coarse sea salt.

Serves 8

3 cups all-purpose flour
½ teaspoon salt
2 teaspoons rapid-rise yeast
1 cup lukewarm water
3 tablespoons olive oil
1 small red onion
leaves from 1 large rosemary sprig
1 teaspoon coarse sea salt

1 Sift the flour and salt into a large mixing bowl. Stir in the yeast, then make a well in the middle of the dry ingredients. Pour in the water and 2 tablespoons of the oil. Mix well, adding a little more water if the mixture seems too dry.

2 Transfer the dough to a lightly floured surface and knead for about 10 minutes, until smooth and elastic.

3 Place the dough in a greased bowl, cover and leave in a warm place for about 1 hour, until doubled in size. Punch down and knead the dough for 2–3 minutes.

4 Grease a baking sheet. Roll out the dough to a large circle about ½ inch thick, and transfer to the greased baking sheet. Brush with the remaining oil.

5 Halve the onion and slice it into thin wedges. Sprinkle over the dough with the rosemary and sea salt, pressing lightly.

6 Using a finger, make deep indentations in the dough. Cover with greased plastic wrap. Then allow to rise in a warm place for 30 minutes. Preheat the oven to 425°F. Remove the plastic wrap and bake for 25–30 minutes, until golden.

NUTRITION NOTES

Per portion

Calories	191
Fat	4.72g
Saturated Fat	0.68g
Cholesterol	0
Fiber	1.46g

Onion Focaccia

This pizza-like flatbread is characterized by its soft, dimpled surface.

Serves 8
6 cups bread flour
½ teaspoon salt
½ teaspoon sugar
1 tablespoon rapid-rise yeast
4 tablespoons extra virgin olive oil
2 cups lukewarm water

To finish
2 red onions, thinly sliced
3 tablespoons extra virgin olive oil
1 tablespoon coarse salt

1 Sift the flour, salt and sugar into a large bowl. Stir in the yeast, oil and water and mix to a dough using a blunt knife. (Add a little extra water if the dough is dry.)

2 Turn out onto a lightly floured surface and knead for about 10 minutes, until smooth and elastic. Put the dough in a clean, lightly oiled bowl and cover with plastic wrap. Set aside to rise in a warm place until doubled in bulk.

3 Place two 10-inch plain metal flan rings on baking sheets. Oil the sides of the rings and the baking sheets.

4 Preheat the oven to 400°F. Halve the dough and roll each piece to a 10-inch round. Press into the rings, cover with a dampened dishcloth and let rise for 30 minutes.

5 Make deep holes, about 1 inch apart, in the dough. Cover and let sit for another 20 minutes.

6 Sprinkle the onions on top and drizzle with the oil. Sprinkle with the salt, then a little cold water, to prevent a crust from forming.

7 Bake for about 25 minutes, sprinkling with water again during cooking. Cool on a wire rack.

NUTRITION NOTES

Per portion

Calories	202
Fat	3.28g
Saturated Fat	0.46g
Cholesterol	0
Fiber	22.13g

Sun-Dried Tomato Braid

This is a marvelous Mediterranean-flavored bread to serve at a summer buffet or barbecue.

Serves 8–10

1¼ cups warm water
1 teaspoon active dry yeast
pinch of sugar
2 cups whole-wheat flour
2 cups bread flour
1 teaspoon salt
¼ teaspoon freshly ground black pepper
⅔ cup drained sun-dried tomatoes in oil, chopped, plus 1 tablespoon oil from the jar
¼ cup freshly grated Parmesan cheese
2 tablespoons sun-dried tomato pesto
1 teaspoon coarse sea salt

Cook's Tip
If you can't find sun-dried tomato pesto, use 2 tablespoons chopped fresh basil mixed with 1 tablespoon sun-dried tomato paste.

NUTRITION NOTES
Per portion

Calories	294
Fat	12.12g
Saturated Fat	2.13g
Cholesterol	3.4mg
Fiber	3.39g

1 Put half the warm water in a jug. Sprinkle the yeast on top. Add the sugar, mix well and let sit for 10 minutes.

2 Put the whole-wheat flour in a mixing bowl. Sift in the white flour, salt and pepper. Make a well in the center and add the yeast mixture, sun-dried tomatoes, oil, Parmesan, pesto and the remaining water. Gradually incorporate the flour and mix to a soft dough, adding a little extra water if necessary.

3 Transfer the dough to a floured surface and knead for 5 minutes, until smooth and elastic. Return to the clean bowl, cover with a damp dish towel and set aside in a warm place to rise for about 2 hours, until doubled in bulk. Lightly grease a baking sheet.

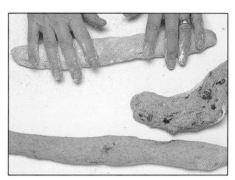

4 Transfer the dough to a lightly floured surface and knead for a few minutes. Divide the dough into three equal pieces and shape each piece into a 12-inch-long sausage.

5 Dampen the ends of the three sausages. Press them together at one end, braid them loosely, then press them together at the other end. Place on the baking sheet, cover and let sit in a warm place for 30 minutes, until well risen. Preheat the oven to 425°F.

6 Sprinkle the braid with the coarse sea salt. Bake for 10 minutes, then lower the temperature to 400°F and bake for another 15–20 minutes, or until the loaf sounds hollow when tapped on the bottom. Cool on a wire rack.

Saffron Focaccia

A dazzling yellow bread with a distinctive flavor.

Serves 10

pinch of saffron threads
⅔ cup boiling water
2 cups all-purpose flour
½ teaspoon salt
1 teaspoon rapid-rise yeast
1 tablespoon olive oil

For the topping

2 garlic cloves, sliced
1 red onion, cut into thin wedges
rosemary sprigs
12 black olives, pitted and
coarsely chopped
1 tablespoon olive oil

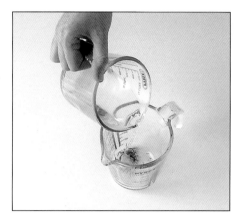

1 Infuse the saffron in the boiling water. Let sit until cooled to lukewarm.

2 Place the flour, salt, yeast and olive oil in a food processor. Turn on and gradually add the saffron and its liquid until the dough forms a ball.

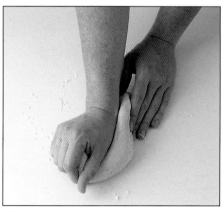

3 Transfer to a floured board and knead for 10–15 minutes. Place in a bowl, cover and let rise for 30–40 minutes, until doubled in size.

4 Punch down the risen dough on a lightly floured surface and roll out into an oval shape ½ inch thick. Place on a lightly greased baking sheet and let rise for 20–30 minutes.

5 Preheat the oven to 400°F. Use your fingers to press small indentations in the dough.

6 Cover with the topping ingredients, brush lightly with olive oil, and bake for about 25 minutes, or until the loaf sounds hollow when tapped on the bottom. Allow to cool.

NUTRITION NOTES

Per portion

Calories	104
Fat	15.91g
Saturated Fat	4g
Cholesterol	0
Fiber	9.4g

Spinach and Bacon Bread

This bread is so tasty that it is a good idea to make double the quantity and freeze some of the loaves.
Use lean Canadian bacon for the best possible flavor with the minimum amount of fat.

Serves 8

scant 2 cups warm water
2 teaspoons active dry yeast
pinch of sugar
1 tablespoon olive oil
1 onion, chopped
4 ounces Canadian bacon
slices, chopped
8 ounces chopped spinach, thawed
if frozen
6 cups bread flour
1½ teaspoons salt
1½ teaspoons grated nutmeg
¼ cup grated reduced-fat
Cheddar cheese

Cook's Tip
If using frozen spinach, be sure
to squeeze out any excess liquid
or the resulting dough will be
too sticky.

NUTRITION NOTES
Per portion

Calories	172
Fat	2.17g
Saturated Fat	0.36g
Cholesterol	1.97mg
Fiber	1.68g

1 Put the water in a bowl. Sprinkle the yeast on top and add the sugar. Mix well and let sit for 10 minutes. Lightly grease two 9-inch cake pans.

2 Heat the oil in a frying pan and fry the onion and Canadian bacon for 10 minutes, until golden brown. Meanwhile, if using frozen spinach, drain it thoroughly.

3 Sift the flour, salt and nutmeg into a mixing bowl and make a well in the center. Add the yeast mixture. Tip in the fried bacon and onion (with the oil), then add the spinach. Gradually incorporate the flour mixture and mix to a soft dough.

4 Transfer the dough to a floured surface and knead for 5 minutes, until smooth and elastic. Return to the clean bowl, cover with a damp dish towel and set aside in a warm place to rise for about 2 hours, until doubled in bulk.

5 Transfer the dough to a floured surface, knead briefly, then divide it in half. Shape each half into a ball, flatten slightly and place in a pan, pressing the dough so that it extends to the edges. Mark each loaf into eight wedges and sprinkle with the cheese. Cover loosely with a plastic bag and set aside in a warm place until well risen. Preheat the oven to 400°F.

6 Bake the loaves for 25–30 minutes, or until they sound hollow when they are tapped underneath. Transfer to a wire rack to cool.

Prosciutto and Parmesan Bread

This nourishing bread is almost a meal in itself.

Serves 8
2 cups whole-wheat flour
2 cups self-rising
white flour
3 teaspoons baking powder
1¼ teaspoons salt
1 teaspoon black pepper
3 ounces prosciutto, chopped
2 tablespoons freshly grated Parmesan
cheese
2 tablespoons chopped fresh parsley
3 tablespoons Dijon mustard
1½ cups buttermilk
skim milk, to glaze

NUTRITION NOTES

Per portion

Calories	250
Fat	3.65g
Saturated Fat	1.3g
Cholesterol	7.09mg
Fiber	3.81g

1 Preheat the oven to 400°F. Flour a baking sheet. Place the whole-wheat flour in a bowl and sift in the white flour, baking powder and salt. Add the pepper and the prosciutto. Set aside about 1 tablespoon of the grated Parmesan and stir the rest into the flour mixture with the parsley. Make a well in the center.

2 Mix the mustard and buttermilk, pour into the flour and quickly mix to a soft dough.

3 Transfer the dough to a floured surface and knead briefly. Shape into an oval loaf, brush with milk and sprinkle with the reserved Parmesan cheese. Put the loaf on the prepared baking sheet.

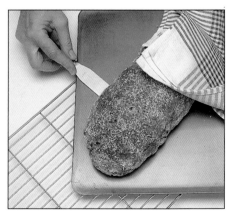

4 Bake the loaf for 25–30 minutes, or until it sounds hollow when tapped on the bottom. Let cool before serving.

Caraway Breadsticks

Ideal to nibble with drinks, these can be made with all sorts of other seeds—
try cumin seeds, poppy seeds or celery seeds.

1 Grease two baking sheets. Put the warm water in a jug. Sprinkle the yeast on top. Add the sugar, mix well and let sit for 10 minutes.

2 Sift the flour and salt into a mixing bowl, stir in the caraway seeds and make a well in the center. Add the yeast mixture and gradually incorporate the flour to make a soft dough, adding a little water if necessary.

3 Preheat the oven to 425°F. Transfer the dough to a lightly floured surface and knead for 5 minutes, until smooth. Divide the mixture into 20 pieces and roll each piece into a 12-inch stick.

4 Arrange the sticks on the baking sheets, leaving room between them to allow for rising.

5 Bake the breadsticks for about 10–12 minutes, until golden brown. Cool on the baking sheets.

Makes about 20
⅔ cup warm water
½ teaspoon active dry yeast
pinch of sugar
2 cups all-purpose flour
½ teaspoon salt
2 teaspoons caraway seeds

NUTRITION NOTES
Per portion
Calories	45
Fat	0.24g
Saturated Fat	0.02g
Cholesterol	0
Fiber	0.3g

Cheese and Onion Sticks

An extremely tasty bread that is very good with soups or salads. Use an extra-sharp cheese to give plenty of flavor without piling on the fat.

Serves 8–12

1¼ cups warm water
1 teaspoon active dry yeast
pinch of sugar
1 tablespoon sunflower oil
1 red onion, finely chopped
4 cups bread flour
1 teaspoon salt
1 teaspoon dry mustard
3 tablespoons chopped fresh herbs,
such as thyme, parsley, marjoram or
sage
¾ cup grated reduced-fat Cheddar
cheese

Cook's Tip
To make Onion and Coriander Sticks, omit the cheese, herbs and mustard. Add 1 tablespoon ground coriander and 3 tablespoons chopped fresh cilantro instead.

NUTRITION NOTES
Per portion

Calories	210
Fat	3.16g
Saturated Fat	0.25g
Cholesterol	3.22mg
Fiber	1.79g

1 Put the water in a jug. Sprinkle the yeast on top. Add the sugar, mix well and let sit for 10 minutes.

2 Heat the oil in a small frying pan and fry the onion until it is well colored.

3 Stir together the flour, salt and mustard in a mixing bowl, then add the chopped herbs. Set aside 2 tablespoons of the cheese. Stir the rest into the flour mixture and make a well in the center. Add the yeast mixture with the fried onions and oil, then gradually incorporate the flour and mix to a soft dough, adding extra water if necessary.

4 Transfer the dough to a floured surface and knead for 5 minutes, until smooth and elastic. Return to the clean bowl, cover with a damp dish towel and set aside in a warm place to rise for about 2 hours, until doubled in bulk. Lightly grease a baking sheet.

5 Transfer the dough to a floured surface, knead briefly, then divide the mixture in half and roll each piece into a 12-inch-long stick. Place each stick on the baking sheet and make diagonal cuts along the top.

6 Sprinkle the sticks with the reserved cheese. Cover and let sit for 30 minutes, until well risen. Preheat the oven to 425°F. Bake the sticks for 25 minutes, or until they sound hollow when tapped on the bottom.

Saffron and Basil Breadsticks

Saffron lends its delicate aroma and flavor, as well as rich yellow color, to these tasty breadsticks.

Makes 32

generous pinch of saffron strands
2 tablespoons hot water
4 cups bread flour
1 teaspoon salt
2 teaspoons rapid-rise yeast
1¼ cups lukewarm water
3 tablespoons olive oil
3 tablespoons chopped fresh basil

1 Infuse the saffron strands in the hot water for 10 minutes.

2 Sift the flour and salt into a large mixing bowl. Stir in the yeast, then make a well in the center of the dry ingredients. Pour in the lukewarm water and saffron liquid and start to mix a little.

3 Add the oil and basil and continue to mix to a soft dough.

4 Turn out and knead the dough on a lightly floured surface for about 10 minutes, until smooth and elastic. Place in a greased bowl, cover with plastic wrap and let sit for about 1 hour, until it has doubled in size.

5 Punch down and knead the dough on a lightly floured surface for 2–3 minutes.

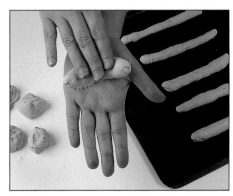

6 Preheat the oven to 425°F. Divide the dough into 32 pieces and shape into long sticks. Place well apart on greased baking sheets, then leave for another 15–20 minutes, until they become puffy. Bake for about 15 minutes, until crisp and golden. Serve warm.

NUTRITION NOTES

Per portion

Calories	59
Fat	1.3g
Saturated Fat	0.17g
Cholesterol	0
Fiber	0.4g

Cook's Tip

Use powdered saffron if saffron strands are not available. Turmeric is an inexpensive alternative: It imparts a lovely gold color, but its flavor is not as delicate.

Olive and Herb Bread

Olive breads are popular all over the Mediterranean. For this Greek recipe, use rich, oily olives or those marinated in herbs, not canned ones.

Serves 20

2 red onions, thinly sliced
2 tablespoons olive oil
8 ounces (1½ cups) pitted black or green olives
7 cups bread flour
1½ teaspoons salt
4 teaspoons rapid-rise yeast
3 tablespoons roughly chopped parsley, cilantro or mint
2 cups lukewarm water

NUTRITION NOTES

Per portion

Calories	157
Fat	2.9g
Saturated Fat	0.41g
Cholesterol	0
Fiber	1.8g

1 Fry the onions in the oil until soft. Roughly chop the olives.

2 Put the flour, salt, yeast and parsley, cilantro or mint in a large bowl with the olives and fried onions and pour in the water. Mix to a dough using a blunt knife, adding a little more water if the mixture feels dry.

3 Transfer to a lightly floured surface and knead for about 10 minutes. Put in a clean bowl, cover with plastic wrap and set aside in a warm place until doubled in bulk.

4 Preheat the oven to 425°F. Lightly grease two baking sheets. Turn out the dough onto a floured surface and cut in half. Shape into two rounds and place on the baking sheets. Cover loosely with lightly oiled plastic wrap and let sit until doubled in size.

5 Slash the tops of the loaves with a knife, then bake for about 40 minutes, or until the loaves sound hollow when tapped on the bottom. Transfer to a wire rack to cool.

Variation

Shape the dough into 16 small rolls. Slash the tops as above and reduce the cooking time to 25 minutes.

Tomato Breadsticks

Once you've tried this simple recipe, you'll never buy commercially made breadsticks again.
Serve as a snack, or with aperitifs and a dip before a meal.

1 Place the flour, salt and yeast in a food processor. Add the honey and olive oil and, with the machine running, gradually pour in the water (you may not need it all, as flours vary). Stop adding water as soon as the dough starts to cling together. Process for 1 minute more.

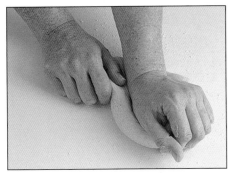

2 Transfer the dough to a floured board and knead for 3–4 minutes, until springy and smooth.

3 Knead in the chopped sun-dried tomatoes. Form into a ball and place in a lightly oiled bowl. Let rise for 5 minutes.

4 Preheat the oven to 300°F. Divide the dough into 16 pieces and roll each piece into an 11 x ½-inch stick. Place on a lightly oiled baking sheet and let rise in a warm place for 15 minutes.

Cook's Tip
Instead of sun-dried tomatoes, you could try making these breadsticks with reduced-fat Cheddar cheese, sesame seeds or herbs.

5 Brush the sticks with milk and sprinkle with poppy seeds. Bake for 30 minutes. Let cool on a wire rack.

Makes 16
2 cups all-purpose flour
½ teaspoon salt
½ teaspoon rapid-rise yeast
1 teaspoon honey
1 teaspoon olive oil
⅔ cup warm water
6 halves sun-dried tomatoes in olive oil, drained and chopped
1 tablespoon skim milk
2 teaspoons poppy seeds

NUTRITION NOTES
Per portion
Calories	82
Fat	3.53g
Saturated Fat	0.44g
Cholesterol	0
Fiber	0.44g

Sourdough Bread

Sourdough bread has a slightly sour, tangy flavor created by using a special yeast starter as the leavener.

Serves 10
3 cups flour
1 tablespoon salt
½ cup lukewarm water

For the starter
1 teaspoon active dry yeast
¾ cup lukewarm water
½ cup flour

Cook's Tip
The starter can be chilled for up to one week, but must be brought back to room temperature before using.

NUTRITION NOTES
Per portion	
Calories	179
Fat	0.7g
Saturated Fat	0.1g
Cholesterol	0
Fiber	1.6g

1 For the starter, combine the yeast and water, stir and let sit for 15 minutes to dissolve.

2 Sprinkle in the flour and whisk until it forms a batter; it does not have to be smooth. Cover and let rise in a warm place for at least 24 hours, or preferably 2–4 days, before using.

3 For the bread, combine the flour and salt in a large bowl. Make a well in the center and add the starter and water. With a wooden spoon, stir from the center, incorporating more flour with each turn, to obtain a rough dough.

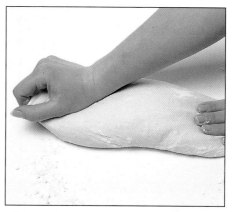

4 Transfer the dough to a floured surface. To knead, push the dough away from you with the palm of your hand, then fold it toward you, and push it away again. Repeat the process until the dough has become smooth and elastic.

5 Place in a clean bowl, cover, and let rise in a warm place until doubled in volume, about 2 hours. Lightly grease an 8 x 4-inch bread pan.

6 Punch down the dough with your fist. Knead briefly, then form into a loaf shape and place in the pan, seam side down. Cover with a plastic bag, and let rise in a warm place until the dough rises above the rim of the pan, about 1½ hours.

7 Preheat the oven to 425°F. Dust the top of the loaf with flour, then score lengthwise. Bake for 15 minutes. Lower the heat to 375°F and bake for about 30 minutes more, or until the bottom sounds hollow when tapped.

Potato Bread

A recipe for a traditional loaf—one that is low in fat.

Serves 16

4 teaspoons active dry yeast
1 cup lukewarm skim milk
½ pound peeled potatoes, boiled
(reserve 1 cup of potato
cooking liquid)
2 tablespoons oil
4 teaspoons salt
6–6½ cups all-purpose flour

NUTRITION NOTES

Per portion

Calories	177
Fat	1.7g
Saturated Fat	0.2g
Cholesterol	0.2mg
Fiber	1.5g

1 Combine the yeast and the milk in a large bowl and let sit to dissolve for about 15 minutes. Mash the potatoes.

2 Add the potatoes, oil and salt to the yeast mixture and mix well. Stir in 1 cup of the cooking water, then stir in the flour, 1 cup at a time, to form a stiff dough.

3 Transfer to a floured surface and knead until smooth and elastic. Return to the bowl, cover and set aside in a warm place until doubled in size, 1–1½ hours. Punch down, then let rise for another 40 minutes.

4 Grease two 9 x 5-inch loaf pans. Roll the dough into 20 small balls. Place two rows of balls in each pan. Let sit until the dough has risen above the rim of the pans.

5 Preheat the oven to 400°F. Bake for 10 minutes, then lower the heat to 375°F and bake for about 40 minutes, or until the bottoms of the loaves sound hollow when tapped. Cool on a rack.

Irish Soda Bread

This is a solid bread—delicious with lunch or dinner.

1 Preheat the oven to 400°F. Grease a baking sheet.

2 Sift the flours, baking soda and salt together in a bowl. Make a well in the center and add the butter or margarine and buttermilk. Working outward from the center, stir with a fork until a soft dough is formed.

3 With floured hands, gather the dough into a ball.

4 Transfer to a floured surface and knead for 3 minutes. Shape the dough into a large round.

5 Place on the baking sheet. Cut a cross in the top with a sharp knife.

6 Dust with flour. Bake until brown, 40–50 minutes. Transfer to a wire rack to cool.

Serves 10
2 cups all-purpose flour,
plus 1 tablespoon for dusting
1 cup whole-wheat flour
1 teaspoon baking soda
1 teaspoon salt
2 tablespoons butter or margarine, at room temperature
1½ cups buttermilk

NUTRITION NOTES
Per portion

Calories	188
Fat	3.3g
Saturated Fat	0.7g
Cholesterol	1 mg
Fiber	2.3g

Brown Soda Bread

This is very easy to make—simply mix and bake. Instead of yeast, baking soda and cream of tartar are the rising agents. This is an excellent recipe for those new to bread making.

Serves 20
4 cups all-purpose flour
4 cups whole-wheat flour
2 teaspoons salt
1 tablespoon baking soda
4 teaspoons cream of tartar
2 teaspoons sugar
4 tablespoons butter
up to 3¾ cups buttermilk or skim milk
extra whole-wheat flour, to sprinkle

NUTRITION NOTES

Per portion	
Calories	185
Fat	2.9g
Saturated Fat	0.53g
Cholesterol	1.1mg
Fiber	2.8g

1 Lightly grease a baking sheet. Preheat the oven to 375°F.

2 Sift all the dry ingredients into a large bowl, pouring any bran from the flour back into the bowl.

3 Rub the butter into the flour mixture, then add enough buttermilk or milk to make a soft dough. You may not need all of it, so add it cautiously.

4 Knead the dough lightly until smooth—do not overknead—then transfer to the baking sheet and shape into a large round about 2 inches thick.

5 Using the floured handle of a wooden spoon, make a large cross on top of the dough. Sprinkle with a little extra whole-wheat flour.

6 Bake for 40–50 minutes, until risen and firm. Cool for 5 minutes before transferring to a wire rack to cool further.

Sage Soda Bread

This wonderful loaf is not like bread made with yeast. It has a velvety texture and a powerful sage aroma.

1 Preheat the oven to 425°F. Sift the dry ingredients into a mixing bowl.

2 Stir in the sage and add enough buttermilk to make a soft dough.

3 Shape the dough into a round loaf with your hands and place on a lightly oiled baking sheet.

4 Cut a deep cross in the top. Bake for about 40 minutes, until the loaf is well risen and sounds hollow when tapped on the bottom. Allow to cool on a wire rack.

Serves 10

1½ cups whole-wheat flour
1 cup bread flour
½ teaspoon salt
1 teaspoon baking soda
2 tablespoons shredded fresh sage or
2 teaspoons dried sage
scant 1¼ cups buttermilk

NUTRITION NOTES

Per portion

Calories	125
Fat	9.2g
Saturated Fat	0.2g
Cholesterol	0.7mg
Fiber	2.81g

Cook's Tip

As an alternative to the sage, try using either finely chopped rosemary or thyme.

Spiral Herb Bread

An attractive and delicious bread that is ideal for serving with a salad for a healthy lunch.

Serves 20
2 teaspoons active dry yeast
2½ cups lukewarm water
3⅔ cups bread flour
1 tablespoon salt
2 tablespoons sunflower margarine
large bunch of parsley, finely chopped
bunch of scallions, chopped
garlic clove, finely chopped
salt and freshly ground black pepper
1 egg, lightly beaten
skim milk, for glazing

NUTRITION NOTES

Per portion
Calories	85
Fat	1.22g
Saturated Fat	0.49g
Cholesterol	7.24mg
Fiber	1.54g

1 Combine the yeast with approximately ¼ cup of the water, stir and let sit to dissolve. Mix together the flour and salt in a large bowl. Make a well in the center and pour in the yeast mixture and the remaining water. With a wooden spoon, stir from the center, working outward, to obtain a rough dough.

2 Transfer the dough to a floured surface and knead until smooth and elastic. Return to the bowl, cover with a plastic bag, and let sit for about 2 hours, until doubled in volume.

3 Meanwhile, combine the margarine, parsley, scallions and garlic in a large frying pan. Cook over low heat, stirring, until softened. Season with salt and pepper and set aside.

4 Grease two 9 x 5-inch loaf pans. When the dough has risen, cut in half and roll each half into a rectangle measuring about 14 x 9 inches. Brush both with the beaten egg. Divide the herb mixture between the two, spreading just up to the edges.

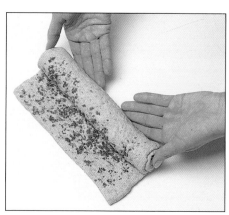

5 Roll up to enclose the filling and pinch the short ends to seal. Place in the pans, seam side down. Cover the dough with a clean dish towel and leave undisturbed in a warm place until the dough rises above the rims of the pans.

6 Preheat the oven to 375°F. Brush the loaves with milk and bake for about 55 minutes, until the bottoms sound hollow when tapped. Cool on a wire rack.

Walnut Bread

Delicious at any time of day, this bread may be eaten plain or topped with low-fat cream cheese.

1 Mix together the flours and salt in a large bowl. Make a well in the center and pour in 1 cup of the water, the honey and the yeast. Set aside until the yeast dissolves and the mixture is frothy.

2 Add the remaining water. With a wooden spoon, stir from the center, incorporating flour with each turn, to obtain a smooth dough. Add more flour to the bowl if the dough is too sticky, and use your hands if the dough becomes too stiff to stir.

3 Transfer to a floured board and knead, adding flour if necessary, until the dough is smooth and elastic. Place in a greased bowl and roll the dough around in the bowl to coat thoroughly all over.

6 Preheat the oven to 425°F. With a sharp knife, score the top of the loaf and brush with the egg glaze. Bake for 15 minutes. Lower the temperature to 375°F and bake for about 40 minutes, or until the bottom of the loaf sounds hollow when tapped. Allow to cool.

Serves 10

3⅔ cups whole-wheat flour
1¼ cups bread flour
2½ teaspoons salt
2¼ cups lukewarm water
1 tablespoon honey
1 tablespoon rapid-rise yeast
1¼ cups walnut pieces, plus more for decorating
1 egg, beaten, for glazing

NUTRITION NOTES

Per portion

Calories	285
Fat	10.93g
Saturated Fat	1.2g
Cholesterol	7.7mg
Fiber	4.7g

4 Cover with a plastic bag and let sit in a warm place until doubled in volume, about 1½ hours.

5 Punch down the dough very firmly and knead in the walnuts. Shape the dough into a round loaf and place on a greased baking sheet. Press in the walnut pieces to decorate the top. Cover loosely with a damp dish towel and set aside in a warm place for 25–30 minutes, until doubled in size.

Oatmeal Bread

A healthy bread with a delightfully crumbly texture, due to the inclusion of rolled oats.

Serves 20

2 cups skim milk
2 tablespoons low-fat margarine
1¼ cups dark brown sugar
2 teaspoons salt
1 tablespoon rapid-rise yeast
¼ cup lukewarm water
3½ cups rolled oats
4–6 cups bread flour

NUTRITION NOTES

Per portion

Calories	228
Fat	3.44g
Saturated Fat	1.19g
Cholesterol	3.9mg
Fiber	2.41g

1 Scald the milk. Remove from the heat and stir in the margarine, sugar and salt. Let sit until lukewarm.

2 Combine the yeast and lukewarm water in a large bowl and let sit until the yeast is dissolved and the mixture is frothy. Stir in the milk mixture.

3 Add 2½ cups of the oats and enough flour to obtain a soft, pliable dough.

4 Transfer to a floured surface and knead until smooth and elastic.

5 Place the dough in a greased bowl, cover with a plastic bag, and let sit for 2–3 hours, until doubled in volume. Grease a large baking sheet.

6 Transfer the dough to a lightly floured surface and divide in half.

7 Shape into rounds. Place on the baking sheet, cover with a damp dish towel and let rise for about 1 hour, until doubled in volume.

8 Preheat the oven to 400°F. Score the tops of the loaves and sprinkle with the remaining oats. Bake for 45–50 minutes, until the bottoms sound hollow when tapped. Cool on wire racks.

Zucchini and Walnut Loaf

A moist and crunchy loaf—a real treat.

1 Preheat the oven to 350°F. Grease the bottom and sides of a 2-pound loaf pan and line with waxed paper.

2 Beat the eggs and sugar together and gradually add the oil.

3 Sift the flour into a bowl together with the baking powder, baking soda, cinnamon and allspice.

4 Mix into the egg mixture with the rest of the ingredients, reserving 1 tablespoon of the sunflower seeds for the top.

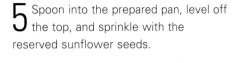

5 Spoon into the prepared pan, level off the top, and sprinkle with the reserved sunflower seeds.

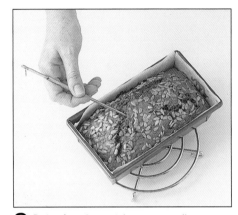

6 Bake for about 1 hour, or until a skewer inserted into the center comes out clean. Let cool slightly, then turn out onto a wire cooling rack.

Serves 10

3 eggs
½ cup light brown sugar
¼ cup sunflower oil
1½ cups whole-wheat flour
1 teaspoon baking powder
1 teaspoon baking soda
1 teaspoon ground cinnamon
½ teaspoon ground allspice
½ tablespoon green cardamom pods, seeds removed and crushed
5 ounces (1 cup) coarsely grated zucchini
2 ounces (¼ cup) walnuts, chopped
2 ounces (¼ cup) sunflower seeds

NUTRITION NOTES
Per portion
Calories	307
Fat	20.19g
Saturated Fat	2.64g
Cholesterol	65.45mg
Fiber	2.86g

Italian Flatbread with Sage

This bread is perfect served hot to accompany a pasta supper.

Serves 10

2 teaspoons active dry yeast
1 cup lukewarm water
3 cups all-purpose flour
2 teaspoons salt
5 tablespoons extra virgin olive oil
12 fresh sage leaves, chopped

NUTRITION NOTES

Per portion

Calories	205
Fat	6.1g
Saturated Fat	0.6g
Cholesterol	0
Fiber	1.4g

1 Combine the yeast and water, stir and let sit for 15 minutes to dissolve.

2 Mix the flour and salt in a large bowl, and make a well in the center.

3 Stir in the yeast mixture and 4 table-spoons of the oil. Stir from the center, incorporating flour with each turn, to obtain a rough dough.

4 Transfer to a floured surface and knead until smooth and elastic. Place in a lightly oiled bowl. Cover and let rise in a warm place until doubled in volume, about 2 hours.

5 Preheat the oven to 400°F and place a baking sheet in the center of the oven.

6 Punch down the dough. Knead in the sage leaves, then roll into a 12-inch round. Let rise slightly.

7 Dimple the surface all over with your finger. Drizzle the remaining oil on top. Slide a floured board under the bread, carry to the oven, and slide off onto the hot baking sheet. Bake for about 35 minutes, or until golden brown. Allow to cool on a wire rack.

Zucchini Yeast Bread

The grated zucchini gives extra moisture to this tasty loaf.

1 In a colander, alternate layers of grated zucchini and salt. Let sit for 30 minutes, then squeeze out the moisture with your hands.

2 Combine the yeast with ¼ cup of the lukewarm water, stir and let sit for 15 minutes to dissolve the yeast.

3 Place the zucchini, yeast and flour in a bowl. Stir together and add just enough of the remaining water to obtain a rough dough.

4 Transfer to a floured surface and knead until smooth and elastic. Return the dough to the bowl, cover with a plastic bag, and set aside to rise in a warm place until doubled in volume, about 1½ hours.

5 Grease a baking sheet. Punch down the risen dough with your fist and knead into a tapered cylinder. Place on the baking sheet, cover and let rise in a warm place until doubled in volume, about 45 minutes.

6 Preheat the oven to 425°F. Brush the bread with olive oil and bake for 40–45 minutes, or until the loaf is a golden color. Cool on a rack before serving.

Serves 10

1 pound (3½ cups) grated zucchini
2 tablespoons salt
2 teaspoons active dry yeast
1¼ cups lukewarm water
3½ cups all-purpose flour
olive oil, for brushing

NUTRITION NOTES

Per portion

Calories	191
Fat	1.2g
Saturated Fat	0.2g
Cholesterol	0
Fiber	2g

Rosemary Bread

Sliced thinly, this herb bread is delicious with soup for a light meal.

Serves 10

¼ ounce rapid-rise yeast
1½ cups whole-wheat flour
1½ cups self-rising flour
2 teaspoons butter, melted, plus extra
to grease bowl and pan
¼ cup warm water
1 cup skim milk, at room temperature
1 tablespoon sugar
1 teaspoon salt
1 tablespoon sesame seeds
1 tablespoon dried chopped onion·
1 tablespoon fresh rosemary leaves,
plus extra to decorate
4 ounces (1 cup) cubed Cheddar cheese
coarse salt, to decorate

NUTRITION NOTES

Per portion

Calories	188
Fat	5.6g
Saturated Fat	1.7g
Cholesterol	6mg
Fiber	2.2g

1 Mix the yeast with the flours in a large mixing bowl. Add the melted butter. Stir in the warm water, milk, sugar, salt, sesame seeds, onion and rosemary. Knead thoroughly until quite smooth.

2 Flatten the dough, then add the cheese cubes. Quickly knead them in until they are well combined.

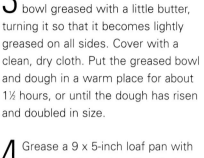

3 Place the dough into a large clean bowl greased with a little butter, turning it so that it becomes lightly greased on all sides. Cover with a clean, dry cloth. Put the greased bowl and dough in a warm place for about 1½ hours, or until the dough has risen and doubled in size.

4 Grease a 9 x 5-inch loaf pan with the remaining butter. Punch down the dough to remove some of the air, and shape it into a loaf. Put the loaf into the pan, cover with the clean cloth used earlier and set aside for about 1 hour, until it has doubled in size once again. Preheat the oven to 375°F.

5 Bake for 30 minutes. During the last 5–10 minutes of baking, cover the loaf with aluminum foil to prevent it from becoming too dark. Remove from the loaf pan and let cool on a wire rack. Decorate with rosemary leaves and coarse salt sprinkled on top.

Dill Bread

Herb bread makes a tasty change at any mealtime.

1 Mix together the yeast, water and sugar in a large bowl and let sit for 15 minutes to dissolve.

2 Stir in 3 cups of the flour. Cover and let rise in a warm place for 45 minutes.

3 Cook the onion in 1 tablespoon of the oil until soft. Set aside to cool, then stir into the yeast mixture. Stir the dill, eggs, cottage cheese, salt and remaining oil into the yeast mixture. Gradually add the remaining flour until too stiff to stir.

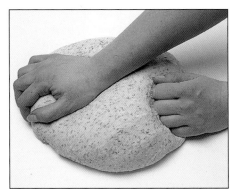

4 Transfer to a floured surface and knead until smooth and elastic. Place in a bowl, cover, and leave to rise until doubled in volume, for 1–1½ hours.

5 Grease a large baking sheet. Cut the dough in half and shape into two rounds. Set aside to rise in a warm place for 30 minutes.

6 Preheat the oven to 375°F. Score the tops, brush with the milk, and bake until browned, about 50 minutes. Cool on a wire rack.

Serves 20

4 teaspoons active dry yeast
2 cups lukewarm water
2 tablespoons sugar
7½ cups all-purpose flour
½ onion, chopped
4 tablespoons oil
1 large bunch of dill, finely chopped
2 eggs, lightly beaten
4 ounces (½ cup) cottage cheese
4 teaspoons salt
milk, for glazing

NUTRITION NOTES

Per portion

Calories	237
Fat	3.7g
Saturated Fat	0.6g
Cholesterol	20mg
Fiber	1.8g

Naan

This is a particularly easy recipe for making naan, an Indian bread. Always serve naan warm, preferably straight from the broiler, or wrap in foil until you are ready to serve.

Makes 6
1 teaspoon sugar
1 teaspoon active dry yeast
⅔ cup warm water
2 cups all-purpose flour
1 teaspoon ghee or butter
1 teaspoon salt
4 tablespoons low-fat margarine, melted
1 teaspoon poppy seeds

NUTRITION NOTES

Per portion
Calories	177
Fat	5.07g
Saturated Fat	1.24g
Cholesterol	0.5mg
Fiber	0.2g

---

1 Put the sugar and yeast in a small bowl, add the warm water and mix well until the yeast has dissolved. Let sit for 10 minutes, or until the mixture becomes frothy.

2 Place the flour in a large mixing bowl, make a well in the middle and add the ghee or butter and salt, then pour in the yeast mixture.

3 Mix well, using your hands, to make a dough, adding some more water if the dough is too dry. Turn out onto a floured surface and knead for about 5 minutes, or until smooth.

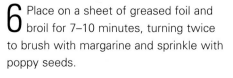

4 Place the dough back in the clean bowl, cover with foil and let rise in a warm place for 1½ hours, or until doubled in size.

5 Preheat the broiler to very hot. Transfer the dough to a floured surface and knead for another 2 minutes. Break off small balls with your hand and roll into rounds about 5 inches in diameter and 1 inch thick.

6 Place on a sheet of greased foil and broil for 7–10 minutes, turning twice to brush with margarine and sprinkle with poppy seeds.

Whole-Wheat Chapatis

These Indian breads are best served hot from the pan—but can be kept warm in foil.

1 Place the flour and salt in a mixing bowl. Make a well in the middle and gradually stir in the water, mixing well with your fingers.

2 Form a supple dough and knead for 7–10 minutes. Ideally, cover with plastic wrap and set aside for 15–20 minutes. If time is short, roll out right away.

3 Divide the dough into 8–10 equal portions. Roll out each piece to a round on a well-floured surface.

4 Place a heavy frying pan over high heat. When steam rises from it, lower the heat to medium and add the first chapati to the pan.

5 When the chapati begins to bubble, turn it over. Press down with a clean dish towel or a flat spoon and turn once again. Remove from the pan and keep warm in foil. Repeat the process until all the chapatis are cooked.

Makes 8–10
2 cups whole-wheat flour
½ teaspoon salt
¾ cup water

NUTRITION NOTES
Per portion

Calories	87
Fat	0.62g
Saturated Fat	0.08g
Cholesterol	0
Fiber	1.3g

Tea Breads

These light and tasty tea
breads use the natural
sweetness of fruit and
honey for a midafternoon
energy-boosting treat that
won't weigh you down.

Banana and Cardamom Bread

The combination of banana and cardamom is delicious in this soft-textured moist loaf.
It is perfect for teatime, served with low-fat spread or jam.

Serves 6

⅔ cup warm water
1 teaspoon active dry yeast
pinch of sugar
10 cardamom pods
3½ cups bread flour
1 teaspoon salt
2 tablespoons malt extract
2 ripe bananas, mashed
1 teaspoon sesame seeds

Cook's Tip

Make sure the bananas are really ripe, so that they impart maximum flavor to the bread. If you prefer, place the dough in one piece in a 1-pound loaf pan and bake for an extra 5 minutes. In addition to being low in fat, bananas are a good source of potassium; they therefore make an ideal nutritious, low-fat snack.

NUTRITION NOTES

Per portion

Calories	299
Fat	1.55g
Saturated Fat	0.23g
Cholesterol	0
Fiber	2.65g

1 Put the warm water in a small bowl. Sprinkle the yeast on top. Add the sugar, mix well and let sit for 10 minutes.

2 Split the cardamom pods. Remove the seeds and chop them finely.

3 Sift the flour and salt into a mixing bowl and make a well in the center. Add the yeast mixture with the malt extract, chopped cardamom seeds and bananas.

4 Gradually incorporate the flour and mix to a soft dough, adding a little extra water if necessary. Turn the dough out onto a floured surface and knead for about 5 minutes, until smooth and elastic. Return to the clean bowl, cover with a damp dish towel and allow to rise for about 2 hours, until doubled in bulk.

5 Grease a baking sheet. Turn the dough out onto a floured surface, knead briefly, then divide into three pieces and shape into a braid. Place the braid on the baking sheet and cover loosely with a plastic bag (ballooning it to trap the air). Let sit until well risen. Preheat the oven to 425°F.

6 Brush the braid lightly with water and sprinkle with the sesame seeds. Bake for 10 minutes, then lower the oven temperature to 400°F. Cook for 15 minutes more, or until the loaf sounds hollow when it is tapped on the bottom. Cool on a wire rack.

Banana Orange Loaf

For the best banana flavor and a good, moist texture, make sure the bananas are very ripe for this cake.

Serves 8

¾ cup whole-wheat flour
¾ cup all-purpose flour
1 teaspoon baking powder
1 teaspoon apple pie spice
3 tablespoons sliced hazelnuts, toasted
2 large ripe bananas
1 egg
2 tablespoons sunflower oil
2 tablespoons honey
finely grated rind and juice of
1 small orange
4 orange slices, halved
2 teaspoons confectioners' sugar

NUTRITION NOTES

Per portion

Calories	217
Fat	7.59g
Saturated Fat	0.92g
Cholesterol	24.06mg
Fiber	2.46g

1 Preheat the oven to 350°F.

2 Brush a 4-cup loaf pan with sunflower oil and line the bottom with baking parchment.

3 Sift the flours with the baking powder and spice into a large bowl, adding any bran that is caught in the sieve. Stir in the toasted hazelnuts.

4 Peel and mash the bananas. Beat together with the egg, oil, honey and orange rind and juice. Stir evenly into the dry ingredients.

5 Spoon into the prepared pan and smooth the top. Bake for 40–45 minutes, or until firm and golden brown. Turn out and cool on a wire rack. Sprinkle the orange slices with the confectioners' sugar and broil until golden. Use to decorate the cake.

Cook's Tip

If you plan to keep the loaf for more than two or three days, omit the orange slices, brush with honey and sprinkle with sliced hazelnuts.

Apple, Apricot and Walnut Loaf

Serve warm and store what is left in an airtight container.

1 Preheat the oven to 350°F. Line and grease a 2-pound loaf pan.

2 Sift the flour, baking powder and salt into a large mixing bowl, then pour the bran remaining in the sieve into the mixture. Add the margarine, sugar, eggs, orange rind and juice. Stir, then beat with a handheld electric mixer until smooth.

3 Stir in the walnuts and apricots. Peel, quarter, and core the apple, chop it roughly and add it to the mixture. Stir, then spoon into the prepared pan and level the top.

4 Bake for 1 hour, or until a skewer inserted into the center of the loaf comes out clean. Cool in the pan for about 5 minutes, then turn out onto a wire rack and peel off the lining paper.

Serves 10–12
2 cups whole-wheat flour
1 teaspoon baking powder
pinch of salt
8 tablespoons (1 stick) sunflower margarine
1 cup light brown sugar
2 eggs, lightly beaten
grated rind and juice of 1 orange
2 ounces (½ cup) chopped walnuts
2 ounces (½ cup) dried apricots, chopped
1 large cooking apple

NUTRITION NOTES

Per portion

Calories	290
Fat	14.5g
Saturated Fat	2.5g
Cholesterol	43.5mg
Fiber	1.6g

Banana and Ginger Tea Bread

Serve this tea bread in slices with low-fat spread. The preserved ginger adds an interesting flavor.

Serves 6–8

1½ cups self-rising flour
1 teaspoon baking powder
3 tablespoons soft margarine
⅓ cup dark brown sugar
⅓ cup drained preserved
ginger, chopped
4 tablespoons skim milk
2 ripe bananas, mashed

NUTRITION NOTES

Per portion
Calories	214
Fat	5.16g
Saturated Fat	0.96g
Cholesterol	0.57mg
Fiber	1.59g

1 Preheat the oven to 350°F. Grease and line a 1-pound loaf pan. Sift the flour and baking powder into a mixing bowl.

2 Rub in the margarine until the mixture resembles bread crumbs.

3 Stir in the sugar. Add the ginger, milk and bananas and mix to a soft dough.

4 Spoon into the prepared pan and bake for 40–45 minutes, or until an inserted skewer comes out clean. Run a metal spatula around the edges to loosen, then turn the tea bread out onto a wire rack and let it cool.

Glazed Banana Spice Loaf

For an instant variation, omit the glaze and spread with Quark for a teatime treat.

1 Preheat the oven to 350°F. Line a 9 x 5-inch loaf pan with waxed paper and grease.

2 With a fork, mash the banana in a bowl. Set aside.

3 With an electric mixer, cream the butter and sugar until light and fluffy. Add the eggs, one at a time, beating to blend well after each addition. Sift together the flour, salt, baking soda, nutmeg, allspice and cloves. Add to the butter mixture and stir to combine well.

4 Add the sour cream, banana and vanilla extract and mix just enough to blend. Pour into the prepared pan.

5 Bake for 45–50 minutes, until the top springs back when touched lightly. Allow to cool in the pan for 10 minutes before turning out onto a wire rack.

6 For the glaze, combine the confectioners' sugar and lemon juice, then stir until smooth. To glaze, set the rack over a baking sheet. Pour the glaze over the top of the bread and allow to set.

Serves 10

1 large ripe banana
8 tablespoons (1 stick) butter, at room temperature
¾ cup granulated sugar
2 eggs, at room temperature
1½ cups all-purpose flour
1 teaspoon salt
1 teaspoon baking soda
½ teaspoon grated nutmeg
¼ teaspoon ground allspice
¼ teaspoon ground cloves
¾ cup sour cream
1 teaspoon vanilla extract

For the glaze

1 cup confectioners' sugar
1–2 tablespoons fresh lemon juice

NUTRITION NOTES

Per portion

Calories	362
Fat	14.1g
Saturated Fat	4.3g
Cholesterol	49mg
Fiber	0.8g

Orange Honey Bread

A moist and fruity bread made using naturally sweet ingredients.

Serves 10

2½ cups all-purpose flour
2½ teaspoons baking powder
½ teaspoon baking soda
½ teaspoon salt
2 tablespoons margarine
1 cup honey
1 egg, at room temperature,
lightly beaten
1½ tablespoons grated orange rind
¾ cup freshly squeezed orange juice
3 ounces (¾ cup) walnuts, chopped

NUTRITION NOTES

Per portion
Calories	300
Fat	11.2g
Saturated Fat	1.49g
Cholesterol	19.5mg
Fiber	1.6g

1 Preheat the oven to 325°F. Sift together the flour, baking powder, baking soda and salt.

2 Line the bottom and sides of a 9 x 5-inch loaf pan with waxed paper and grease.

3 With an electric mixer, cream the margarine until soft. Stir in the honey until blended, then stir in the egg. Add the orange rind and stir to combine.

4 Fold the flour mixture into the honey and egg mixture in three batches, alternating with the orange juice. Stir in the walnuts.

5 Pour into the pan and bake for 60–70 minutes, or until a skewer inserted into the center comes out clean. Allow to stand for 10 minutes before turning out onto a rack to cool.

Applesauce Bread

Apples and spices such as cinnamon and nutmeg are a match made in heaven.

1 Preheat the oven to 350°F. Line the bottom and sides of a 9 x 5-inch loaf pan with waxed paper and grease.

2 Break the egg into a bowl and beat lightly. Stir in the baked apples, butter or margarine and both sugars. Set aside.

3 In another bowl, sift together the flour, baking powder, baking soda, salt, cinnamon and nutmeg. Fold the dry ingredients into the applesauce mixture in three batches.

4 Stir in the currants or raisins and chopped pecans.

5 Pour into the prepared pan and bake for about 1 hour, or until a skewer inserted into the center comes out clean. Let stand for 10 minutes before transferring to a wire rack to cool.

Serves 10

1 egg
8 ounces (1 cup) baked apples
4 tablespoons butter or margarine, melted
½ cup dark brown sugar, firmly packed
¼ cup granulated sugar
2 cups all-purpose flour
2 teaspoons baking powder
½ teaspoon baking soda
½ teaspoon salt
1 teaspoon ground cinnamon
½ teaspoon grated nutmeg
3 ounces (½ cup) currants or raisins
6 ounces (½ cup) pecans, chopped

NUTRITION NOTES

Per portion
Calories	299
Fat	11.2g
Saturated Fat	1.2g
Cholesterol	20mg
Fiber	1.8g

Cranberry Orange Bread

Try this classic muffin combination in a tasty tea bread.

Serves 10

2 cups all-purpose flour
½ cup sugar
1 tablespoon baking powder
½ teaspoon salt
grated rind of 1 large orange
⅔ cup fresh orange juice
2 eggs, lightly beaten
6 tablespoons butter or margarine
6 ounces (1½ cups) fresh cranberries
2 ounces (½ cup) walnuts, chopped

NUTRITION NOTES

Per portion

Calories	285
Fat	14g
Saturated Fat	2.3g
Cholesterol	39mg
Fiber	2g

1 Preheat the oven to 350°F. Line the bottom and sides of a 9 x 5-inch loaf pan with waxed paper and grease. Sift the flour, sugar, baking powder and salt into a mixing bowl.

2 Stir the orange rind into the dry ingredients.

3 Make a well in the center and add the orange juice, eggs and melted butter or margarine. Stir from the center until the ingredients are blended; do not overmix.

4 Add the cranberries and walnuts and stir until blended. Transfer the batter to the prepared pan and bake for 45–50 minutes, or until a skewer inserted into the center comes out clean.

5 Let cool in the pan for 10 minutes before transferring to a wire rack to cool completely. Serve thinly sliced, toasted or plain, with butter or cream cheese and jam.

Pear and Golden Raisin Tea Bread

This is an ideal tea bread to make when pears are plentiful—an excellent use for windfalls.

1 Preheat the oven to 350°F. Grease and line a 1-pound loaf pan with baking parchment. Put the oats in a bowl with the sugar, pour the pear or apple juice and oil over them, mix well and let stand for 15 minutes.

2 Quarter, core and coarsely grate the pears. Add the fruit to the oat mixture with the flour, golden raisins, baking powder, apple pie spice and egg, then mix together thoroughly.

3 Spoon the mixture into the prepared loaf pan and level the top. Bake for 50–60 minutes, or until a skewer inserted into the center comes out clean.

4 Transfer the tea bread to a wire rack and peel off the lining paper. Allow to cool completely.

Cook's Tip
Health food stores sell concentrated pear and apple juice, ready for diluting as required.

Serves 6–8
¼ cup rolled oats
¼ cup light brown sugar
2 tablespoons pear or apple juice
2 tablespoons sunflower oil
1 large or 2 small pears
1 cup self-rising flour
4 ounces (¾ cup) golden raisins
½ teaspoon baking powder
2 teaspoons apple pie spice
1 egg

NUTRITION NOTES
Per portion

Calories	200
Fat	4.61g
Saturated Fat	0.79g
Cholesterol	27.5mg
Fiber	1.39g

Dried Fruit Loaf

Dried fruit is a healthy sweet treat, and delicious in this loaf.

Serves 10

15 ounces (2½ cups) mixed dried fruit,
such as currants, raisins, chopped
dried apricots and
dried cherries
1¼ cups cold strong black tea
1 cup dark brown sugar, firmly packed
grated rind and juice of 1 small orange
grated rind and juice of 1 lemon
1 egg, lightly beaten
1¾ cups all-purpose flour
1 tablespoon baking powder
⅛ teaspoon salt

NUTRITION NOTES

Per portion
Calories	298
Fat	1.1g
Saturated Fat	0.2g
Cholesterol	19.2mg
Fiber	1.8g

1 In a bowl, toss together all the dried fruit, pour the tea over it and let soak overnight.

2 Preheat the oven to 350°F. Line the bottom and sides of a 9 x 5-inch loaf pan with waxed paper and grease.

3 Strain the fruit, reserving the liquid. In a bowl, combine the sugar, orange and lemon rind and fruit.

4 Pour the orange and lemon juice into a measuring jug; if the quantity is less than 1 cup, make up with the soaking liquid.

5 Stir the citrus juices and egg into the dried fruit mixture.

6 In another bowl, sift together the flour, baking powder and salt. Stir into the fruit mixture until blended.

7 Transfer to the prepared pan and bake for 1¼ hours, or until a skewer inserted into the center comes out clean. Allow to stand for 10 minutes before turning out.

Date and Nut Malt Loaf

A moist loaf—perfect for brown-bag lunches.

1 Sift the flours and salt into a large bowl, adding any bran from the sieve. Stir in the sugar and yeast.

2 Put the butter or margarine in a small pan with the molasses and malt extract. Stir over low heat until melted. Let cool, then combine with the milk.

3 Stir the liquid into the dry ingredients and knead thoroughly for 15 minutes, until the dough is elastic. (If you have a dough blade on your food processor, follow the manufacturer's instructions for timing.)

4 Knead in the fruits and nuts. Transfer the dough to an oiled bowl, cover with plastic wrap, and let sit in a warm place for about 1½ hours, until the dough has doubled in size.

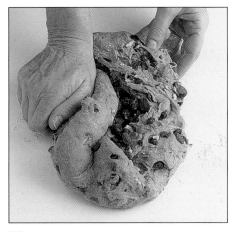

5 Grease two 1-pound loaf pans. Punch down the dough and knead lightly. Divide in half, form into loaves and place in the pans. Cover and let sit in a warm place for about 30 minutes, until risen. Meanwhile, preheat the oven to 375°F.

6 Bake for 35–40 minutes, until the loaves are well risen and sound hollow when tapped on the bottom. Cool on a wire rack. Brush with honey while warm.

Serves 16

2 cups bread flour
2 cups whole-wheat flour
1 teaspoon salt
6 tablespoons brown sugar
1 teaspoon rapid-rise yeast
4 tablespoons butter or margarine
1 tablespoon molasses
4 tablespoons malt extract
1 cup tepid milk
4 ounces (½ cup) chopped dates
3 ounces (½ cup) golden raisins
3 ounces (½ cup) raisins
2 ounces (½ cup) chopped nuts
2 tablespoons clear honey, to glaze

NUTRITION NOTES
Per portion
Calories	216
Fat	5.57g
Saturated Fat	2.46g
Cholesterol	9.45mg
Fiber	2.8g

Malt Loaf

This is a rich and sticky loaf. If it lasts long enough to go stale, try toasting it for a delicious teatime treat.

Serves 8
⅔ cup warm skim milk
1 teaspoon active dry yeast
pinch of granulated sugar
3 cups all-purpose flour
½ teaspoon salt
2 tablespoons light brown sugar
6 ounces (generous 1 cup) golden raisins
1 tablespoon sunflower oil
3 tablespoons malt extract

For the glaze
2 tablespoons granulated sugar
2 tablespoons water

Cook's Tip
To make buns, divide the dough into 10 pieces, shape into rounds, leave to rise, then bake for about 15–20 minutes. Brush with the glaze while still hot.

NUTRITION NOTES
Per portion

Calories	279
Fat	2.06g
Saturated Fat	0.33g
Cholesterol	0.38mg
Fiber	1.79g

1 Place the warm milk in a bowl. Sprinkle the yeast on top and add the sugar. Let sit for 30 minutes, until frothy. Mix the flour and salt in a mixing bowl, stir in the brown sugar and golden raisins and make a well in the center.

2 Add the yeast mixture with the oil and malt extract. Gradually incorporate the flour and mix to a soft dough, adding a little extra milk if necessary.

3 Turn out onto a floured surface and knead for about 5 minutes, until smooth and elastic. Grease a 1-pound loaf pan.

4 Shape the dough and place it in the prepared loaf pan. Cover with a damp dish towel and let sit in a warm place for 1–2 hours, until the dough is well risen. Preheat the oven to 375°F.

5 Bake the loaf for 30–35 minutes, or until it sounds hollow when tapped on the bottom.

6 Meanwhile, prepare the glaze by dissolving the sugar in the water in a small pan. Bring to the boil, stirring, then lower the heat and simmer for 1 minute. Place the loaf on a wire rack and brush with the glaze while still hot. Leave the loaf to cool before serving.

Lemon Walnut Bread

This is a light and tangy tea bread.

Serves 10

8 tablespoons (1 stick) butter or margarine, at room temperature
½ cup sugar
2 eggs, at room temperature, separated
grated rind of 2 lemons
2 tablespoons fresh lemon juice
1½ cups self-rising flour
2 teaspoons baking powder
½ cup milk
6 ounces (½ cup) walnuts, chopped
⅛ teaspoon salt

NUTRITION NOTES

Per portion
Calories	229
Fat	11.1g
Saturated Fat	1.77g
Cholesterol	39.1mg
Fiber	1g

1 Preheat the oven to 350°F. Line the bottom and sides of a 9 x 5-inch loaf pan with waxed paper and grease.

2 With an electric mixer, cream the butter or margarine with the sugar until light and fluffy.

3 Beat the egg yolks into the creamed butter and sugar.

4 Add the lemon rind and juice and stir until blended. Set aside.

5 In another bowl, sift together the flour and baking powder three times. Fold into the butter mixture in three batches, alternating with the milk. Fold in the chopped walnuts and set the mixture aside.

6 Beat the egg whites and salt until stiff peaks form. Fold a large dollop of the egg whites into the walnut mixture to lighten it. Carefully fold in the remaining egg whites until just blended.

7 Pour the batter into the prepared pan and bake for 45–50 minutes, or until a skewer inserted into the center of the loaf comes out clean. Let stand for 5 minutes before turning out onto a rack to cool completely.

Apricot Nut Loaf

An excellent high-fiber fruit and nut combination.

1 Preheat the oven to 350°F. Line the bottom and sides of a 9 x 5-inch loaf pan with waxed paper and grease.

2 Place the apricots in a bowl and add lukewarm water to cover. Allow to stand for 30 minutes.

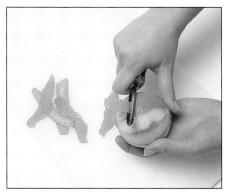

3 With a vegetable peeler, remove the orange rind, leaving the pith.

4 With a sharp knife, finely chop the orange rind strips.

5 Drain the apricots and chop coarsely. Place in a bowl with the orange rind and raisins. Set aside.

6 Squeeze the peeled orange. Measure the juice and add enough hot water to make ¾ cup liquid.

7 Pour the orange juice mixture over the apricot mixture. Stir in the sugar, oil and eggs. Set aside.

8 In another bowl, sift together the flour, baking powder, salt and baking soda. Fold the flour mixture into the apricot mixture in three batches.

9 Stir in the walnuts. Spoon the batter into the prepared pan and bake for 55–60 minutes, or until a skewer inserted into the center of the loaf comes out clean. If the loaf browns too quickly, protect the top with foil. Cool in the pan for 10 minutes before transferring to a wire rack to cool completely.

Serves 10

6 ounces (¾ cup) dried apricots
1 large orange
3 ounces (½ cup) raisins
⅔ cup sugar
⅓ cup oil
2 eggs, lightly beaten
2¼ cups all-purpose flour
2 teaspoons baking powder
½ teaspoon salt
1 teaspoon baking soda
2 ounces (½ cup) walnuts, chopped

NUTRITION NOTES

Per portion

Calories	324
Fat	11.2g
Saturated Fat	1.5g
Cholesterol	38mg
Fiber	2.5g

Date-Nut Bread

A little brandy gives this tea bread an extra-rich flavor.

Serves 10

5 ounces (1 cup) pitted dates, chopped
¾ cup boiling water
4 tablespoons unsalted butter, at room temperature
¼ cup dark brown sugar, firmly packed
¼ cup granulated sugar
1 egg, at room temperature
2 tablespoons brandy
1⅓ cups plain flour
2 teaspoons baking powder
½ teaspoon salt
generous ¾ teaspoon freshly grated nutmeg
3 ounces (¾ cup) pecans, coarsely chopped

NUTRITION NOTES

Per portion

Calories	258
Fat	13.8g
Saturated Fat	1.1g
Cholesterol	20mg
Fiber	1.3g

1 Place the dates in a bowl and pour the boiling water over them. Set aside to cool to lukewarm.

2 Preheat the oven to 350°F. Line the bottom and sides of a 9 x 5-inch loaf pan with waxed paper and grease.

3 With an electric mixer, cream the butter and sugars until they are light and fluffy. Beat in the egg and brandy, then set aside.

4 Sift the flour, baking powder, salt and nutmeg together three times.

5 Fold the dry ingredients into the sugar mixture in three batches, alternating with the dates and water.

6 Fold in the pecans. Pour the batter into the prepared pan and bake for 45–50 minutes, or until a skewer inserted into the center comes out clean. Cool in the pan for 10 minutes before transferring to a rack to cool completely.

Prune Bread

A slightly spicy bread that tastes good with savory spreads.

1 Simmer the prunes in water to cover until soft, or soak overnight. Drain, reserving ¼ cup of the soaking liquid. Pit and chop the prunes.

2 Combine the yeast and the reserved prune liquid, stir, and let sit for 15 minutes to dissolve.

3 In a large bowl, stir together the flours, baking soda, salt and pepper. Make a well in the center.

4 Add the chopped prunes, butter and buttermilk. Pour in the yeast mixture. With a wooden spoon, stir from the center, incorporating more flour with each turn, to obtain a rough dough.

5 Transfer to a floured surface and knead until smooth and elastic. Return to the clean bowl, cover with a plastic bag, and set aside to rise in a warm place until doubled in volume, about 1½ hours. Grease a baking sheet.

6 Punch down the dough with your fist, then knead in the walnuts.

7 Shape the dough into a long, cylindrical loaf. Place on the baking sheet, cover loosely, and let rise in a warm place for 45 minutes.

8 Preheat the oven to 425°F. With a sharp knife, score the top deeply. Brush with milk and bake for 15 minutes. Lower the heat to 375°F and bake for about 35 minutes more, until the bottom sounds hollow when tapped. Cool on a wire rack.

Serves 10

8 ounces (1 cup) dried prunes
2 teaspoons active dry yeast
½ cup whole-wheat flour
2½–3 cups all-purpose flour
½ teaspoon baking soda
1 teaspoon salt
1 teaspoon freshly ground black pepper
2 tablespoons butter, at room temperature
¾ cup buttermilk
6 ounces (½ cup) walnuts, chopped
milk, for glazing

NUTRITION NOTES

Per portion

Calories	262
Fat	8.4g
Saturated Fat	1.1g
Cholesterol	1mg
Fiber	2.1g

Swedish Golden Raisin Bread

A lightly sweetened fruit bread that is delicious served warm. It is also excellent toasted and topped with low-fat spread.

Serves 8–10

⅔ cup warm water
1 teaspoon active dry yeast
1 tablespoon honey
2 cups whole-wheat flour
2 cups bread flour
1 teaspoon salt
4 ounces (⅔ cup) golden raisins
2 ounces (½ cup) walnuts, finely chopped
¾ cup warm skim milk, plus extra for glazing

Cook's Tip

To make Apple and Hazelnut Bread, replace the golden raisins with two chopped eating apples and use chopped toasted hazelnuts instead of the walnuts. Add 1 teaspoon ground cinnamon with the flour.

NUTRITION NOTES

Per portion

Calories	273
Fat	4.86g
Saturated Fat	0.57g
Cholesterol	0.39mg
Fiber	3.83g

1 Put the water in a small jug. Sprinkle the yeast on top. Add a few drops of the honey to help activate the yeast, mix well and let stand for 10 minutes.

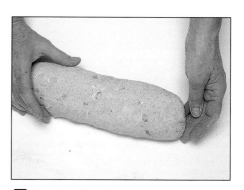

2 Put the flours in a mixing bowl, with the salt and golden raisins. Set aside 1 tablespoon of the walnuts and add the rest to the bowl. Mix together lightly and make a well in the center.

3 Add the yeast and honey mixture to the flour mixture with the milk and remaining honey. Gradually incorporate the flour, mixing to a soft dough; add a little extra water if the dough feels too dry to work with.

4 Turn the dough out onto a floured surface and knead for 5 minutes, until smooth and elastic. Return to the clean bowl, cover with a damp dish towel and set aside in a warm place to rise for about 2 hours, until doubled in bulk. Grease a baking sheet.

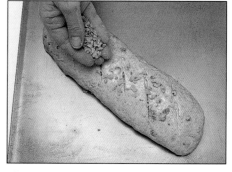

5 Turn the dough out onto a floured surface and form into an 11-inch-long sausage shape. Place on the baking sheet. Make some diagonal cuts down the whole length of the loaf.

6 Brush the loaf with milk, sprinkle with the reserved walnuts and let rise for about 40 minutes. Preheat the oven to 425°F. Bake for 10 minutes. Lower the temperature to 400°F and bake for about 20 minutes more, or until the loaf sounds hollow when tapped on the bottom.

Raisin Bread

Spice, brandy and dried fruit make a good flavor combination.

Serves 20

2 teaspoons active dry yeast
2 cups lukewarm milk
6 ounces (1 cup) raisins
2½ ounces (½ cup) currants
1 tablespoon sherry or brandy
½ teaspoon grated nutmeg
grated rind of 1 large orange
⅓ cup sugar
1 tablespoon salt
8 tablespoons (1 stick) butter, melted
5–6 cups all-purpose flour
1 egg beaten with 1 tablespoon cream,
for glazing

NUTRITION NOTES

Per portion
Calories	235
Fat	5.9g
Saturated Fat	1.2g
Cholesterol	11mg
Fiber	1.4g

1 Stir together the yeast and ½ cup of the milk and let stand for 15 minutes to dissolve.

2 Mix together the raisins, currants, sherry or brandy, nutmeg and orange rind and set aside.

3 In another bowl, mix the remaining milk, sugar, salt and 4 tablespoons of the butter. Add the yeast mixture. With a wooden spoon, stir in 2–3 cups flour, 1 cup at a time, until blended. Add more flour for a stiff dough.

4 Transfer to a floured surface and knead until smooth and elastic. Place in a greased bowl, cover, and let rise in a warm place until doubled in volume, about 2½ hours.

5 Punch down the dough, return to the bowl, cover, and let rise in a warm place for about 30 minutes.

6 Grease two 9 x 5-inch loaf pans. Divide the dough in half and roll each half into a rectangle about 20 x 7 inches.

7 Brush the rectangles with the remaining melted butter. Sprinkle the raisin mixture over them, then roll up tightly from the short end, tucking in the ends slightly as you roll. Place in the prepared pans, cover and let rise until almost doubled in volume.

8 Preheat the oven to 400°F. Brush the top of the loaves with the glaze. Bake for 20 minutes. Lower the heat to 350°F and bake for 25–30 minutes more, or until golden. Cool on wire racks.

Sweet Potato and Raisin Bread

The natural sweetness of sweet potato is used in this healthy loaf.

1 Preheat the oven to 350°F. Grease a 9 x 5-inch loaf pan.

2 Sift the flour, baking powder, salt, cinnamon and nutmeg into a small bowl. Set aside.

3 With an electric mixer, beat the mashed sweet potatoes with the brown sugar, butter or margarine and eggs until well mixed.

4 Add the flour mixture and the raisins. Stir with a wooden spoon until the flour is just mixed in.

5 Transfer the batter to the prepared pan. Bake for 1–1¼ hours, or until a skewer inserted into the center comes out clean.

6 Cool in the pan on a wire rack for 15 minutes, then turn the bread out onto the wire rack and cool completely.

Serves 10

2½ cups all-purpose flour
2 teaspoons baking powder
½ teaspoon salt
1 teaspoon ground cinnamon
½ teaspoon grated nutmeg
1 pound (2 cups) mashed cooked sweet potatoes
½ cup light brown sugar, firmly packed
8 tablespoons (1 stick) butter or margarine, melted and cooled
3 eggs, beaten
3 ounces (½ cup) raisins

NUTRITION NOTES

Per portion

Calories	338
Fat	11.6g
Saturated Fat	2.4g
Cholesterol	59mg
Fiber	2.4g

Cardamom and Saffron Tea Loaf

An aromatic sweet bread ideal for afternoon tea or lightly toasted for breakfast. Using rapid-rise, or easy-blend, yeast makes bread making so simple.

Serves 20

generous pinch of saffron strands
3 cups lukewarm milk
2 tablespoons butter
8 cups bread flour
2 teaspoons rapid-rise yeast
3 tablespoons sugar
6 cardamom pods, seeds extracted
⅔ cup raisins
2 tablespoons honey, plus more for brushing
1 egg, beaten

NUTRITION NOTES

Per portion

Calories	22
Fat	2.1g
Saturated Fat	0.4g
Cholesterol	10mg
Fiber	1.7g

1 Crush the saffron into a cup containing a little of the warm milk and allow to infuse for 5 minutes.

2 Rub the butter into the flour, then mix in the yeast, sugar and cardamom seeds (these may need rubbing to separate them). Stir in the raisins.

3 Beat the remaining milk with the honey and egg, then mix this into the flour along with the saffron milk and strands, stirring well until a firm dough is formed. You may not need all the milk; it depends on the flour.

4 Turn out the dough and knead it on a lightly floured board for about 5 minutes, until smooth.

5 Return the dough to the mixing bowl, cover with oiled plastic wrap and let sit in a warm place until doubled in size. This could take 1–3 hours. Grease a 2-pound loaf pan. Turn the dough out onto a floured board again, punch it down, knead for three minutes, then shape it into a fat roll and fit it into the greased loaf pan.

6 Cover with a sheet of lightly oiled plastic wrap and let stand in a warm place until the dough begins to rise again. Preheat the oven to 400°F. Bake the loaf for 25 minutes, until golden brown and firm on top. Turn the loaf out of the pan and as it cools, brush the top with honey. Slice when cool and spread with butter. It is also good lightly toasted.

Sweet Sesame Loaf

Toasted sesame seeds add a lovely nutty flavor to this loaf.

1 Preheat the oven to 350°F. Line a 10 x 6-inch baking pan, or two small loaf pans, with waxed paper and grease.

2 Reserve 2 tablespoons of the sesame seeds. Spread the rest on a baking sheet and bake until lightly toasted, about 10 minutes. Sift the flour, baking powder and salt into a bowl.

5 Pour into the prepared pan and sprinkle with the reserved sesame seeds.

6 Bake for about 1 hour, or until a skewer inserted into the center comes out clean. Cool in the pan for 10 minutes before turning out.

Serves 10

⅔ cup sesame seeds
2 cups all-purpose flour
2½ teaspoons baking powder
1 teaspoon salt
4 tablespoons butter or margarine, at room temperature
⅔ cup sugar
2 eggs, at room temperature
grated rind of 1 lemon
1½ cups milk

NUTRITION NOTES
Per portion

Calories	133
Fat	5.1g
Saturated Fat	0.9g
Cholesterol	20mg
Fiber	0.7g

3 Stir in the toasted sesame seeds and set aside. With an electric mixer, cream the butter or margarine and sugar together until light and fluffy. Beat in the eggs, then stir in the lemon rind and milk.

4 Pour the milk mixture over the dry ingredients and fold in with a large metal spoon until just blended.

Greek Easter Bread

In Greece, Easter celebrations are very important and involve much preparation in the kitchen. This bread is sold in all the baker's shops and is also made at home. It is traditionally decorated with red-dyed eggs.

Serves 10

1 ounce fresh yeast
½ cup warm milk
6 cups bread flour
2 eggs, beaten
½ teaspoon caraway seeds
1 tablespoon sugar
1 tablespoon brandy
4 tablespoons butter, melted
1 egg white, beaten
½ cup slivered almonds
2–3 hard-boiled eggs, dyed red

NUTRITION NOTES

Per portion

Calories	344
Fat	10.1g
Saturated Fat	3.6g
Cholesterol	89mg
Fiber	2.5g

1 Crumble the yeast into a bowl. Mix with 1–2 tablespoons of warm water, until softened. Add the milk and 1 cup of the flour and mix to a creamy consistency. Cover with a cloth and leave in a warm place to rise for 1 hour.

2 Sift the remaining flour into a large bowl and make a well in the center. Pour the risen yeast into the well, and draw in a little of the flour from the sides. Add the eggs, caraway seeds, sugar and brandy. Incorporate the remaining flour until the mixture begins to form a dough.

3 Mix in the melted butter. Turn out onto a floured surface and knead for about 10 minutes, until the dough becomes smooth. Return to the bowl and cover with a dish towel. Let sit in a warm place for 3 hours.

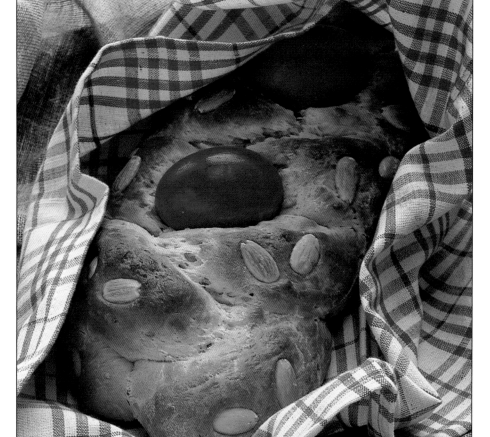

4 Preheat the oven to 350°F. Punch down the dough, turn out onto a floured surface and knead for a minute or two. Divide the dough into three pieces and roll each piece into a long sausage shape. Make a braid as shown above and place the loaf on a greased baking sheet.

5 Tuck the ends under, brush with the egg white and decorate with the slivered almonds. Bake for about 1 hour, until the loaf sounds hollow when tapped on the bottom. Cool on a wire rack. Serve decorated with the hard-boiled eggs.

Orange Wheat Loaf

Perfect just with butter as a breakfast bread or tea bread and great for banana sandwiches.

1 Sift the flour into a large bowl and return any bran caught in the sieve. Add the salt and rub in the butter lightly with your fingertips.

2 Stir in the sugar, yeast and orange rind. Pour the orange juice into a measuring cup and make up to ⅞ cup with hot water (the liquid should not be more than lukewarm).

3 Stir the liquid into the flour and mix to a soft ball of dough. Knead the dough gently on a lightly floured surface until quite smooth.

4 Place the dough in a greased 1-pound loaf pan and set aside in a warm place until nearly doubled in size. Preheat the oven to 425°F.

5 Bake the bread for 30–35 minutes, or until it sounds hollow when tapped on the bottom. Turn out of the pan and cool on a wire rack.

Serves 8

2¼ cups whole-wheat flour
½ teaspoon salt
4 tablespoons butter
2 tablespoons light brown sugar
½ envelope rapid-rise yeast
grated rind and juice of ½ orange

NUTRITION NOTES

Per portion

Calories	144
Fat	3.32g
Saturated Fat	1.82g
Cholesterol	7.19mg
Fiber	3.24g

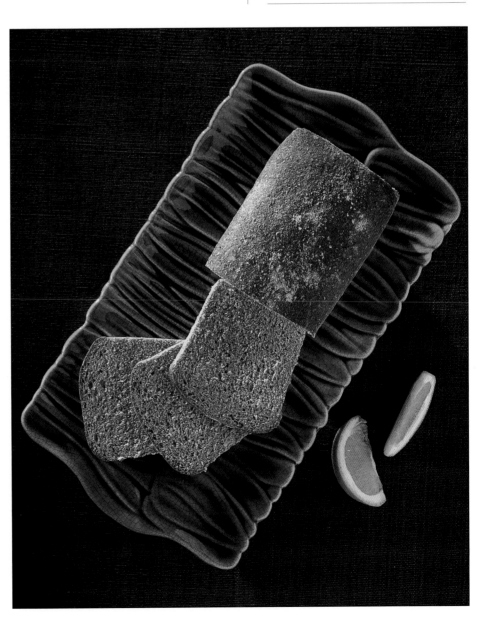

Savory
Baked Goods

Savory baked goods such as pizzas, soufflés, and tartlets are irresistible served warm or piping hot. As an extra bonus, popovers, turnovers and scones are also very quick to make.

Smoked Salmon Pizzettes

Mini pizzas topped with smoked salmon, crème fraîche and lumpfish caviar make
an extra-special party canapé.

Makes 10–12
5-ounce package pizza-dough mix
1 tablespoon snipped
fresh chives
1 tablespoon olive oil
3–4 ounces smoked salmon,
cut into strips
4 tablespoons crème fraîche
2 tablespoons black lumpfish caviar
chives, to garnish

NUTRITION NOTES
Per portion

Calories	126
Fat	2.9g
Saturated Fat	0.8g
Cholesterol	37mg
Fiber	0.9g

1 Preheat the oven to 400°F. Grease two baking sheets. Knead the dough gently, adding the chives until evenly mixed.

2 Roll out the dough on a lightly floured surface to about ⅛ in thick. Using a 3-inch plain round cutter, stamp out 10–12 rounds.

3 Place the rounds well apart on the two baking sheets, prick all over with a fork, then brush with the oil. Bake for 10–15 minutes, until crisp and golden.

4 Arrange the smoked salmon on top, then spoon on the crème fraîche. Spoon a tiny amount of caviar in the center and garnish with chives. Serve immediately.

Calzone

Cut into this folded pizza to reveal a deliciously tempting filling.

1 To make the dough, sift the flour and salt into a bowl and stir in the yeast. Stir in just enough warm water to make a soft dough.

2 Knead for 5 minutes until smooth. Cover and set aside in a warm place for about 1 hour, or until doubled in size.

3 Meanwhile, to make the filling, heat the oil and sauté the onion and zucchini for 3–4 minutes. Remove from the heat and add the tomatoes, cheese, oregano and seasoning.

4 Preheat the oven to 425°F. Knead the dough lightly and divide into four pieces. Roll out each piece on a lightly floured surface to an 8-inch round and place a quarter of the filling on one half of each round.

5 Brush the edges with milk and fold over to enclose the filling. Press firmly to enclose. Brush with milk.

6 Bake on an oiled baking sheet for 15–20 minutes. Serve hot or cold.

Serves 4

4 cups all-purpose flour
pinch of salt
2 teaspoons rapid-rise yeast
about 1½ cups warm water

For the filling

1 teaspoon olive oil
1 medium red onion, thinly sliced
3 medium zucchini, sliced
2 large tomatoes, diced
5 ounces mozzarella cheese, diced
1 tablespoon chopped fresh oregano
salt and freshly ground black pepper
skim milk, to glaze

NUTRITION NOTES

Per portion
Calories	544
Fat	10.93g
Saturated Fat	5.49g
Cholesterol	24.42mg
Fiber	5.09g

Fresh Herb Pizza

Cut this pizza into thin wedges and serve as part of a mixed antipasto.

Serves 8

4 ounces mixed fresh herbs, such as
parsley, basil and oregano
3 garlic cloves, crushed
½ cup heavy cream
1 pizza-dough, round,
10–12 inches in diameter
1 tablespoon garlic oil
1 cup Pecorino cheese, grated
salt and freshly ground black pepper

NUTRITION NOTES

Per portion	
Calories	219
Fat	8.1g
Saturated Fat	3.4g
Cholesterol	27mg
Fiber	1g

1 Preheat the oven to 425°F. Chop the herbs, using a food processor if you have one.

2 In a bowl, mix together the herbs, garlic, cream and seasoning.

3 Brush the pizza crust with the garlic oil, then spread the herb and garlic mixture on top.

4 Sprinkle with the Pecorino cheese. Bake for 15–20 minutes, until crisp and golden and the topping is still moist. Cut into thin wedges to serve.

Mini Pizzas

For a quick supper, try these delicious little pizzas made with fresh and sun-dried tomatoes.

1 Preheat the oven to 400°F. Make up the pizza dough following the instructions on the package.

2 Divide the dough into four pieces and roll each piece out to a 5-inch round. Place on two lightly oiled baking sheets.

3 Place the sun-dried tomatoes and olives in a blender or food processor and blend until smooth. Spread the mixture evenly over the pizza crusts.

4 Top with the tomato slices and crumble the goat cheese over the top. Bake for 10–15 minutes. Sprinkle with the fresh basil and serve at once.

Makes 4

5-ounce package pizza-dough mix
8 halves sun-dried tomatoes in olive oil, drained
2 ounces (½ cup) black olives, pitted
1 large ripe tomato, sliced
2 ounces (¼ cup) goat cheese
2 tablespoons fresh basil leaves

NUTRITION NOTES

Per portion
Calories	326
Fat	11.3g
Saturated Fat	2.8g
Cholesterol	34mg
Fiber	2.8g

Cook's Tip

You can also use loose sun-dried tomatoes (preserved without oil). Let sit in a bowl of warm water for 10–15 minutes to soften, drain and blend with the olives.

Spinach and Feta Triangles

Feta is a medium-fat cheese with a tangy flavor.

Serves 20

2 tablespoons olive oil
2 shallots, finely chopped
1 pound (3 cups) frozen
spinach, thawed
4 ounces (½ cup) feta cheese,
crumbled
1 ounce (⅓ cup) walnut pieces,
chopped
¼ teaspoon grated nutmeg
4 large or 8 small sheets filo pastry
4 tablespoons butter or
margarine, melted
salt and freshly ground black pepper

Cook's Tip

For an alternate filling, omit the spinach and shallots. Use 12 ounces (1½ cups) crumbled goat cheese instead of the feta cheese, and 2 ounces (½ cup) toasted pine nuts instead of the walnuts. Mix the cheese with the olive oil and 1 tablespoon chopped fresh basil. Assemble as above.

NUTRITION NOTES

Per portion

Calories	105
Fat	9g
Saturated Fat	2g
Cholesterol	4mg
Fiber	0.6g

1 Preheat the oven to 400°F.

2 Heat the olive oil in a skillet. Add the shallots and cook until softened, about 5 minutes.

3 A handful at a time, squeeze the excess liquid from the spinach. Add the spinach to the shallots. Increase the heat to high and cook, stirring until all the excess moisture has evaporated, about 5 minutes.

4 Transfer the spinach mixture to a bowl. Cool. Stir in the feta and walnuts. Season with nutmeg, salt and pepper.

5 Lay a filo sheet on a flat surface. (Keep the remaining filo covered with a damp cloth to prevent it from drying out.) Brush with some of the butter or margarine. Lay a second filo sheet on top of the first. With scissors, cut the layered filo pastry lengthwise into 3-inch-wide strips.

6 Place 1 tablespoon of the spinach mixture at the end of one strip of filo pastry.

7 Fold a bottom corner of the pastry over the filling to form a triangle, then continue folding over the pastry strip to the other end. Fill and shape the triangles until all the ingredients are used.

8 Set the triangles on baking sheets and brush with butter. Bake the filo triangles until they are crispy and golden brown, about 10 minutes. Serve hot.

Salmon Parcels

Serve these savory pastries just as they are for a snack, or with a pool of fresh tomato sauce for a special appetizer.

Makes 12

3½-ounce can red or pink salmon
1 tablespoon chopped cilantro
4 scallions, finely chopped
4 sheets filo pastry
sunflower oil, for brushing
scallions and salad leaves,
to serve

NUTRITION NOTES

Per portion

Calories	25
Fat	1.16g
Saturated Fat	0.23g
Cholesterol	2.55mg
Fiber	0.05g

1 Preheat the oven to 400°F. Lightly oil a baking sheet. Drain the salmon, discarding any skin and bones, then place in a bowl.

2 Flake the salmon with a fork and then mix with the cilantro and scallions.

3 Place a single sheet of filo pastry on a work surface and brush lightly with oil. Then place another sheet on top. Cut into six squares measuring about 4 inches a side. Repeat with the remaining pastry to make 12 squares.

4 Place a spoonful of the salmon mixture on each square. Brush the edges of the pastry with oil, then draw together as shown above, pressing to seal. Place the pastries on a baking sheet and bake for 12–15 minutes, until golden. Serve warm, with scallions and salad leaves.

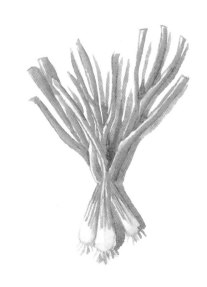

Cook's Tip

When you are using filo pastry, it is important to prevent it from drying out; cover any you are not using with a damp dish towel or plastic wrap.

Tomato Cheese Tarts

These crisp little tartlets are easier to make than they look. They are best eaten fresh from the oven.

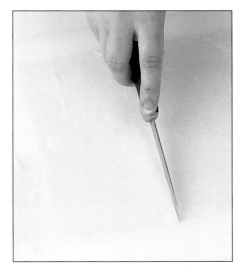

Serves 4
2 sheets filo pastry
1 egg white
½ cup skim-milk soft cheese
handful of fresh basil leaves
3 small tomatoes, sliced
salt and freshly ground black pepper

NUTRITION NOTES

Per portion

Calories	50
Fat	0.33g
Saturated Fat	0.05g
Cholesterol	0.29mg
Fiber	0.25g

1 Preheat the oven to 400°F. Brush the sheets of filo pastry lightly with egg white and cut into sixteen 4-inch squares.

3 Arrange tomatoes on the tarts, add seasoning and bake for 10–12 minutes, until golden. Serve warm.

2 Layer the squares in twos, in eight muffin cups. Spoon the cheese into the pastry shells. Season with black pepper and top with basil leaves.

Red Pepper and Watercress Filo Parcels

Peppery watercress combines well with sweet red pepper in these crisp little pastries.

Makes 8

3 red peppers
1 bunch (6 ounces) watercress
8 ounces (1 cup) ricotta cheese
¼ cup blanched almonds, toasted and chopped
8 sheets filo pastry
2 tablespoons olive oil
salt and freshly ground black pepper

1 Preheat the oven to 375°F. Place the peppers under a hot broiler until blistered and charred. Place in a plastic bag. When cool enough to handle, peel, seed and pat dry on paper towels.

2 Place the peppers and watercress in a food processor and blend until coarsely chopped. Spoon into a bowl.

3 Mix in the ricotta and almonds, and season to taste.

4 Working with one sheet of filo pastry at a time, cut out two 7-inch and two 2-inch squares from each sheet. Brush one large square with a little olive oil and place a second large square at an angle of 45 degrees to form a star shape.

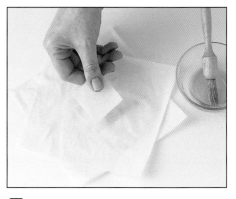

5 Place one of the small squares in the center of the star shape, brush lightly with oil and top with a second small square.

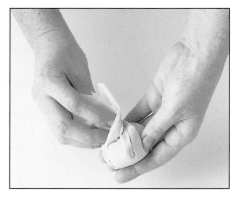

6 Top with one-eighth of the red pepper mixture. Bring the edges together to form a purse shape and twist to seal. Place on a lightly greased baking sheet and cook for 25–30 minutes, until golden.

NUTRITION NOTES

Per portion

Calories	168
Fat	10.2g
Saturated Fat	2.7g
Cholesterol	14mg
Fiber	1.7g

Filo Clam Puffs

Mouthwatering bite-size morsels of seafood.

Makes 54

9 sheets filo pastry, each about 12 x 18 inches
12 ounces (1½ cups) non-fat soft cheese
1 egg, beaten
5 ounces (1 cup) coarsely chopped steamed clams or well-drained canned clams
⅓ cup chopped scallions
2 tablespoons chopped fresh dill
a few drops of hot pepper sauce
8–12 ounces (2–3 sticks) butter or margarine, melted
salt and freshly ground black pepper

NUTRITION NOTES

Per portion

Calories	51
Fat	3.4g
Saturated Fat	0.9g
Cholesterol	5mg
Fiber	0

1 Preheat the oven to 400°F. Stack the sheets of filo pastry and cover with a sheet of plastic wrap.

2 Combine the cheese, egg, clams, scallions, dill, pepper sauce, and some salt and pepper in a bowl. Mix thoroughly.

3 Lay one sheet of filo pastry on the work surface and brush it lightly and evenly with melted butter. Lay another sheet of filo pastry neatly on top and brush it with butter. Cover with a third sheet of filo pastry and brush with butter.

4 Spoon about one-third of the clam mixture in a line along one side of the stacked filo pastry, about 1 inch in from the edge.

5 Fold the nearest long filo pastry edge over the clam filling and continue rolling up. Cut the roll across in half and put the two halves on a buttered baking sheet. Brush the rolls with melted butter.

6 Make two more rolls in the same way and put the halves on the baking sheet. Brush them all with melted butter. Bake until golden brown and crisp, about 20 minutes. Using scissors, cut the rolls across into bite-size pieces. Serve as soon as possible, as an appetizer.

Spinach and Cheese Pie

Using low-fat cottage cheese cuts calories in this delicious pie.

1 Preheat the oven to 375°F.

2 Stack handfuls of spinach leaves, roll them loosely, and cut across the leaves into thin ribbons. Heat the oil in a large saucepan. Add the onion and cook until softened, for about 5 minutes.

3 Add the spinach and oregano and cook for about 5 minutes over high heat, until most of the liquid from the spinach evaporates, stirring frequently. Remove from the heat and let cool. Break the eggs into a bowl and beat. Stir in the cottage cheese and Parmesan cheese and season generously with nutmeg, salt and pepper. Stir in the spinach mixture.

4 Brush a 13 x 9-inch baking dish with some of the butter or margarine. Arrange half of the filo sheets in the bottom of the dish to cover evenly and extend about 1 inch up the sides. Brush with butter.

5 Ladle in the spinach and cheese filling. Cover with the remaining filo pastry, tucking under the edge, neatly.

6 Brush the top with the remaining butter. Score the top with diamond shapes using a sharp knife.

7 Bake for about 30 minutes, or until the pastry is golden brown. Cut into squares and serve hot.

Serves 8

3 pounds (12 cups) fresh spinach, coarse stems removed
2 tablespoons olive oil
1 medium onion, finely chopped
2 tablespoons chopped fresh oregano or 1 teaspoon dried oregano
4 eggs
8 ounces (2 cups) creamed low-fat cottage cheese
6 tablespoons freshly grated Parmesan cheese
grated nutmeg
4 tablespoons butter or margarine, melted
12 sheets filo pastry
salt and freshly ground black pepper

NUTRITION NOTES

Per portion
Calories	299
Fat	16.4g
Saturated Fat	4.4g
Cholesterol	105mg
Fiber	3.8g

Celeriac Gratin

Although celeriac has a rather unattractive appearance with its hard, knobbly skin, it is a vegetable
that has a very delicious sweet and nutty flavor. This is accentuated in this dish by the addition
of the sweet yet nutty Emmenthal cheese.

Serves 4

1 pound celeriac
juice of ½ lemon
2 tablespoons butter or margarine
1 small onion, finely chopped
2 tablespoons all-purpose flour
1¼ cups skim milk
1 ounce (¼ cup) grated Emmenthal
cheese
1 tablespoon capers
salt and cayenne pepper

NUTRITION NOTES

Per portion

Calories	148
Fat	7.7g
Saturated Fat	2.2g
Cholesterol	8mg
Fiber	4.7g

1 Preheat the oven to 375°F. Peel the celeriac and cut into ¼-inch slices, immediately plunging them into a saucepan of cold water with the lemon juice added.

2 Bring the water to a boil and simmer the celeriac for 10–12 minutes, until just tender. Drain and arrange the celeriac in a shallow ovenproof dish.

3 Melt the butter in a small saucepan and fry the onion over gentle heat until soft but not browned. Stir in the flour, cook for 1 minute, then slowly stir in the milk to make a smooth sauce. Stir in the cheese, capers and seasoning to taste, then pour over the celeriac. Cook in the oven for 15–20 minutes, or until the top is golden brown.

Cook's Tip

For a less strongly flavored dish, alternate the layers of celeriac with potatoes. Slice the potatoes, cook until almost tender, then drain well before assembling the dish.

Baked Leeks with Cheese and Yogurt Topping

As with all vegetables, the fresher leeks are, the better their flavor, and the freshest leeks available should be used for this dish. Small, young leeks are best.

1 Preheat the oven to 350°F and butter a shallow ovenproof dish. Trim the leeks, cut a slit from top to bottom and rinse well under cold water.

2 Place the leeks in a saucepan of water, bring to a boil and simmer gently for 6–8 minutes, until just tender. Remove and drain well using a slotted spoon, and arrange in the prepared dish.

3 Beat the eggs with the goat cheese, yogurt and half the Parmesan cheese, and season well with salt and pepper.

4 Pour the cheese and yogurt mixture over the leeks. Mix the bread crumbs and remaining Parmesan cheese together and sprinkle over the sauce. Bake for 30–40 minutes, or until the top is crisp and golden brown.

Serves 4

8 small leeks
2 small eggs or 1 large one, beaten
5 ounces (⅔ cup) fresh goat cheese
⅓ cup low-fat yogurt
2 ounces (⅓ cup) grated Parmesan cheese
⅓ cup fresh white or whole-wheat bread crumbs
salt and freshly ground black pepper

NUTRITION NOTES
Per portion

Calories	259
Fat	15.5g
Saturated Fat	8.2g
Cholesterol	136mg
Fiber	3.8g

Carrot and Cilantro Soufflés

Use tender young carrots for this light-as-air dish.

Serves 4

6–8 carrots
2 tablespoons chopped cilantro
4 eggs, separated
salt and freshly ground black pepper

Cook's Tip
Cilantro tastes wonderful and it's well worth growing your own plant in a window box to ensure a regular supply.

NUTRITION NOTES

Per portion

Calories	115
Fat	5.8g
Saturated Fat	1.55g
Cholesterol	192.5mg
Fiber	2.7g

1 Peel the carrots.

2 Cook in boiling salted water for 20 minutes, or until tender. Drain and process until smooth in a food processor.

3 Preheat the oven to 400°F. Season the puréed carrots well, and stir in the chopped cilantro.

4 Fold the egg yolks into the carrot mixture.

5 In a separate bowl, beat the egg whites until stiff.

6 Fold the egg whites into the carrot mixture and pour into four greased ramekins. Bake for about 20 minutes, or until risen and golden. Serve immediately.

Herb Popovers

Popovers are a muffin-size bread with a crisp brown crust and a delicious moist center.

Makes 12

3 eggs
1 cup skim milk
2 tablespoons butter, melted
¾ cup all-purpose flour
⅛ teaspoon salt
1 small sprig each mixed fresh herbs, such as chives, tarragon, dill and parsley

NUTRITION NOTES

Per portion
Calories	75
Fat	3.5g
Saturated Fat	0.8g
Cholesterol	49mg
Fiber	0.3g

1 Preheat the oven to 425°F. Grease 12 small ramekins or popover cups.

2 With an electric mixer, beat the eggs until blended. Beat in the milk and melted butter.

3 Sift together the flour and salt, then beat into the egg mixture to combine thoroughly.

4 Strip the herb leaves from the stems and chop finely. Mix together and measure out 2 tablespoons. Stir the herbs into the batter.

5 Fill the prepared cups half-full. Bake for 25–30 minutes, or until golden. Do not open the oven door during baking, or the popovers may fall. For drier popovers, pierce each one with a knife after the 30 minutes baking time and bake for 5 minutes more. Serve hot.

Cheese Popovers

Popovers are wonderful when flavored with a strong cheese such as Parmesan.

1 Preheat the oven to 425°F. Grease 12 small ramekins or popover cups.

2 With an electric mixer, beat the eggs until blended. Beat in the milk and melted butter.

3 Sift together the flour, salt and paprika, then beat into the egg mixture. Add the cheese and stir.

4 Fill the prepared cups half-full and bake for 25–30 minutes, or until golden. Do not open the oven door during baking, or the popovers may fall. For drier popovers, pierce each one with a knife after the 30 minutes baking time and bake for 5 minutes more. Serve hot.

Variation

To make Yorkshire Pudding Popovers as an accompaniment for roast beef, omit the cheese and use 4–6 tablespoons of the pan drippings to replace the butter. Put them in the oven in time to serve warm with the beef.

Makes 12

3 eggs
1 cup skim milk
2 tablespoons butter, melted
¾ cup all-purpose flour
¼ teaspoon salt
¼ teaspoon paprika
6 tablespoons freshly grated
Parmesan cheese

NUTRITION NOTES

Per portion
Calories	92
Fat	4.8g
Saturated Fat	1.6g
Cholesterol	52mg
Fiber	0.3g

Pumpkin and Ham Frittata

A frittata is an Italian version of the Spanish omelet, a substantial omelet made from eggs and vegetables. Although frittatas are sometimes eaten cold, this one tastes better warm or hot, served with crusty bread.

Serves 4

2 tablespoons sunflower oil
1 large onion, chopped
1 pound (3 cups) pumpkin, chopped into bite-size pieces
scant 1 cup chicken stock
4 ounces (⅔ cup) chopped smoked ham
6 eggs
2 teaspoons chopped fresh marjoram
salt and freshly ground black pepper

NUTRITION NOTES

Per portion

Calories	231
Fat	15.5g
Saturated Fat	3.5g
Cholesterol	308mg
Fiber	1.8g

1 Preheat the oven to 375°F and oil a large, shallow ovenproof dish. Heat the oil in a large frying pan and sauté the onion for 3–4 minutes until softened.

2 Add the pumpkin and sauté over brisk heat for 3–4 minutes, stirring frequently. Stir in the stock, cover and simmer over gentle heat for 5–6 minutes, until the pumpkin is slightly tender. Add the ham.

3 Pour the mixture into the prepared dish. Beat the eggs with the marjoram and a little seasoning. Pour into the dish and then bake for 20–25 minutes, until the frittata is firm and lightly golden.

Whole-Wheat Herb Triangles

Stuffed with cooked chicken and salad, these make a good lunchtime snack and are also an ideal accompaniment to a bowl of steaming soup.

1 Preheat the oven to 400°F. Lightly flour a baking sheet. Put the whole-wheat flour in a mixing bowl. Sift in the remaining dry ingredients, including the chili powder, then rub in the soft margarine.

3 Carefully cut the dough round into eight wedges, separate them slightly and bake for 15–20 minutes. Transfer to a wire rack to cool. Serve warm or at room temperature.

Makes 8

2 cups whole-wheat flour
1 cup bread flour
1 teaspoon salt
½ teaspoon baking soda
1 teaspoon cream of tartar
½ teaspoon chili powder
4 tablespoons soft margarine
4 tablespoons chopped mixed fresh herbs
1 cup skim milk
1 tablespoon sesame seeds

NUTRITION NOTES

Per portion
Calories	222
Fat	7.22g
Saturated Fat	1.25g
Cholesterol	1.06mg
Fiber	3.54g

2 Add the herbs and milk and mix quickly to a soft dough. Turn out onto a lightly floured surface. Knead only very briefly, or the dough will become tough. Roll out to a 9-inch round and place on the prepared baking sheet. Brush lightly with water and sprinkle evenly with the sesame seeds.

Cook's Tip
To make Sun-dried Tomato Triangles, replace the mixed fresh herbs with 2 tablespoons drained chopped sun-dried tomatoes in oil and add 1 tablespoon each mild paprika, chopped fresh parsley and chopped fresh marjoram.

Curried Crackers

These spicy, crisp little crackers are very low in fat and are ideal for serving with cocktails.

Makes 12
½ cup all-purpose flour
¼ teaspoon salt
1 teaspoon curry powder
¼ teaspoon chili powder
1 tablespoon chopped cilantro
2 tablespoons water

NUTRITION NOTES

Per portion	
Calories	15
Fat	0.11g
Saturated Fat	0.01g
Cholesterol	0
Fiber	0.21g

1 Preheat the oven to 350°F. Sift the flour and salt into a mixing bowl, then add the curry powder and chili powder. Make a well in the center and add the chopped cilantro and water. Gradually incorporate the flour and mix to a firm dough.

2 Turn out onto a lightly floured surface, knead until smooth, then let rest for 5 minutes.

3 Cut the dough into 12 pieces and knead into small balls. Roll each ball out very thinly to a 4-inch round.

4 Arrange the rounds on two ungreased baking sheets, then bake for 15 minutes, turning over once during cooking. Cool on a wire rack.

Variation
Omit the curry and chili powders and add 1 tablespoon caraway, fennel or mustard seeds.

Oatmeal Tartlets with Minted Hummus

Serve these wholesome little tartlets with a crisp salad of romaine lettuce.

1 Preheat the oven to 325°F. Mix together the oatmeal, baking soda and salt in a large bowl. Rub in the butter until the mixture resembles fine crumbs. Stir in the egg yolk and add the milk if the mixture seems too dry.

2 Press into six 3½-inch tartlet pans. Bake for 25–30 minutes. Let cool.

3 Purée the chickpeas, the juice of one lemon, the fromage frais and the tahini in a food processor until smooth. Spoon into a bowl and season with black pepper and more lemon juice to taste. Stir in the chopped mint. Divide among the tartlet molds, sprinkle with pumpkin seeds and dust with paprika.

Serves 6

1⅔ cups medium oatmeal
½ teaspoon baking soda
1 teaspoon salt
2 tablespoons butter
1 egg yolk
2 tablespoons skim milk
14 ounces (2 cups) canned chickpeas, rinsed and drained
juice of 1–2 lemons
1½ cups low-fat fromage frais
4 tablespoons tahini
3 tablespoons chopped fresh mint
2 tablespoons pumpkin seeds
freshly ground black pepper
paprika, for dusting

NUTRITION NOTES

Per portion

Calories	365
Fat	16.8g
Saturated Fat	2.9g
Cholesterol	35mg
Fiber	5.4g

Ham and Tomato Scones

These scones make an ideal accompaniment for soup. Choose a strongly flavored ham,
trimmed of fat, and chop it fairly finely, so that a little goes a long way.

Serves 12
2 cups self-rising flour
1 teaspoon dry mustard
1 teaspoon paprika, plus
extra for sprinkling
½ teaspoon salt
2 tablespoons soft margarine
1 tablespoon snipped fresh basil
1 cup drained sun-dried
tomatoes in oil, chopped
2 ounces (⅓ cup) chopped cooked ham
6–8 tablespoons skim milk, plus extra
for brushing

NUTRITION NOTES
Per portion

Calories	113
Fat	4.23g
Saturated Fat	0.65g
Cholesterol	2.98mg
Fiber	0.65g

1 Preheat the oven to 400°F. Flour a large baking sheet. Sift the flour, mustard, paprika and salt into a bowl. Rub in the margarine until the mixture resembles crumbs.

Cook's Tip
To cut calories and fat, choose dry-packed sun-dried tomatoes and soak them in warm water.

2 Stir in the basil, sun-dried tomatoes and ham, and mix lightly. Pour in enough milk to mix to a soft dough.

3 Turn the dough out onto a lightly floured surface, knead briefly and roll out to an 8 x 6-inch rectangle. Cut into 2-inch squares and arrange on the baking sheet.

4 Brush lightly with milk, sprinkle with paprika and bake for 12–15 minutes. Transfer to a wire rack to cool.

Cheese and Marjoram Scones

With savory toppings, these scones can make a good basis for a light lunch,
served with a crunchy green salad.

1 Gently sift the two kinds of flour into a bowl and add the salt. Cut the butter into small pieces and rub them into the flour until it resembles fine crumbs.

2 Add the mustard, marjoram and grated cheese and mix in sufficient milk to make a soft dough. Knead the dough lightly.

3 Preheat the oven to 425°F. Roll out the dough on a floured surface to ¾ inch thick and cut it out with a 2-inch square cutter. Grease several baking sheets with sunflower oil and place the scones on the sheets. Brush the scones with milk and sprinkle the nuts over the top. Bake for 12 minutes. Serve warm.

Serves 18

1 cup whole-wheat flour
1 cup self-rising flour
pinch of salt
scant 3 tablespoons butter
¼ teaspoon dry mustard
2 teaspoons dried marjoram
½–⅔ cup finely grated Cheddar cheese
½ cup skim milk, or as required
1 teaspoon sunflower oil
⅓ cup pecans or walnuts, chopped

NUTRITION NOTES

Per portion

Calories	90
Fat	4.4g
Saturated Fat	0.6g
Cholesterol	1mg
Fiber	0.5g

Oatcakes

Try serving these oatcakes with reduced-fat hard cheeses. They are also delicious topped with honey for breakfast.

Serves 8

1¼ cups medium oatmeal, plus extra
for sprinkling
½ teaspoon salt
pinch of baking soda
1 tablespoon butter
5 tablespoons water

NUTRITION NOTES

Per portion

Calories	102
Fat	3.43g
Saturated Fat	0.66g
Cholesterol	0.13mg
Fiber	1.49g

1 Preheat the oven to 300°F. Mix the oatmeal with the salt and baking soda in a bowl.

2 Melt the butter with the water in a small saucepan. Bring to a boil, then add to the oatmeal mixture and mix to a moist dough.

3 Turn out the dough onto a surface sprinkled with oatmeal and knead to a smooth ball. Turn a large baking sheet upside down, grease it, sprinkle it lightly with oatmeal and place the ball of dough on top. Sprinkle the dough with oatmeal, then roll out to a 10-inch round.

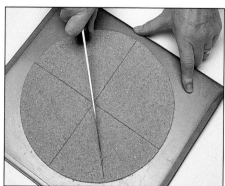

4 Cut the round into eight sections, ease them apart slightly and bake for 50–60 minutes, until crisp. Let cool on the baking sheet, then remove the oatcakes with a metal spatula.

Dill and Potato Cakes

Potato cakes are scrumptious and should be made more often. Try this splendid combination, and you are sure to be converted.

1 Preheat the oven to 450°F. Sift the flour into a bowl and add the butter, salt and dill. Mix in the mashed potato and enough milk to make a soft, pliable dough.

2 Roll out the dough on a well-floured surface until it is fairly thin.

3 Cut into neat rounds with a 3-inch cutter.

4 Grease a baking sheet, place the cakes on it, and bake for 20–25 minutes, until risen and golden.

Serves 10

2 cups self-rising flour
3 tablespoons butter, softened
pinch of salt
1 tablespoon finely chopped fresh dill
scant 1 cup mashed potato, freshly made
2–3 tablespoons milk, as required

NUTRITION NOTES
Per portion

Calories	121
Fat	4g
Saturated Fat	0.8g
Cholesterol	0.4mg
Fiber	0.9g

Chive and Potato Scones

These little scones should be fairly thin, soft in the middle and crisp on the outside. They're extremely quick to make, so serve them for breakfast or lunch.

Makes 20

1 pound (2 large) potatoes
1 cup all-purpose flour, sifted
2 tablespoons olive oil
2 tablespoons snipped chives
salt and freshly ground black pepper
low-fat spread, for topping (optional)

NUTRITION NOTES

Per portion

Calories	50
Fat	1.24g
Saturated Fat	0.17g
Cholesterol	0
Fiber	0.54g

1 Cook the potatoes in a saucepan of boiling salted water for 20 minutes, then drain thoroughly. Return the potatoes to the clean pan and mash them. Preheat a griddle or heavy frying pan over low heat.

2 Add the flour, olive oil and snipped chives with a little salt and pepper to the hot mashed potatoes in the pan. Mix to a soft dough.

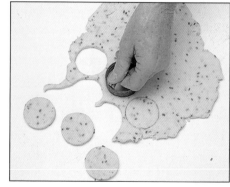

3 Roll out the dough on a well-floured surface to a thickness of ¼ inch and stamp out rounds with a 2-inch pastry cutter.

4 Cook the scones, in batches, on the hot griddle or frying pan for about 10 minutes, until they are golden brown on both sides. Keep the heat low. Top with a little low-fat spread, if you like, and serve immediately.

Cheese and Chive Scones

Try serving these savory scones instead of bread rolls.

1 Preheat the oven to 400°F. Sift the flours, baking powder and salt into a mixing bowl, adding any bran left over from the flour in the sieve.

2 Crumble the feta cheese and rub into the dry ingredients. Stir in the chives, then add the milk and mix to a soft dough.

3 Turn out onto a floured surface and knead lightly until smooth. Roll out to ¾ inch thick and stamp out nine scones with a 2½-inch pastry cutter.

4 Transfer the scones to a nonstick baking sheet. Brush with skim milk, then sprinkle over the cayenne pepper. Bake in the oven for 15 minutes, or until golden.

Makes 9

1 cup self-rising flour
1¼ cups whole-wheat flour
1½ teaspoons baking powder
¾ teaspoon salt
3 ounces (⅓ cup) feta cheese
1 tablespoon snipped fresh chives
⅔ cup skim milk, plus extra
for glazing
¼ teaspoon cayenne pepper

NUTRITION NOTES

Per portion

Calories	121
Fat	2.24g
Saturated Fat	1.13g
Cholesterol	0.4g
Fiber	1.92g

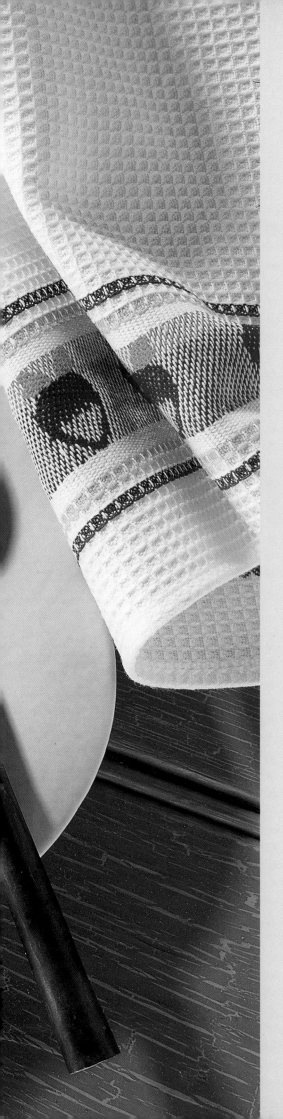

Desserts

Everyone will adore
deliciously light
sweets. Serve a fruity
confection to finish a
family meal, or an
elaborate dessert for
a special occasion.

Chestnut and Orange Roulade

This moist cake is ideal to serve as a dessert.

Serves 8

3 eggs, separated
½ cup granulated sugar
8 ounces (1 cup) canned unsweetened
chestnut purée
grated rind and juice of 1 orange
confectioners' sugar, for dusting

For the filling
1 cup low-fat soft cheese
1 tablespoon honey
1 orange

Cook's Tip
Do not whisk the egg whites too stiffly, or it will be difficult to fold them into the mixture and they will form lumps in the roulade.

NUTRITION NOTES
Per portion

Calories	185
Fat	4.01g
Saturated Fat	1.47g
Cholesterol	76.25mg
Fiber	1.4g

1 Preheat the oven to 350°F. Grease a 12 x 8-inch jelly roll pan and line it with baking parchment. Beat the egg yolks and sugar in a bowl until thick and creamy.

2 Put the chestnut purée in a separate bowl. Beat in the orange rind and juice, then beat the flavored chestnut purée into the egg mixture.

3 Beat the egg whites in a grease-free bowl until fairly stiff. Using a metal spoon, stir a generous spoonful of the whites into the chestnut mixture to lighten it, then fold in the rest. Spoon into the prepared pan and bake for 30 minutes, until firm. Cool for 5 minutes, then cover with a clean damp dish towel until completely cool.

4 Meanwhile, make the filling. Put the soft cheese in a bowl with the honey. Finely grate the orange rind and add to the bowl. Peel away all the pith from the orange, cut the fruit into segments, chop roughly and set aside. Add any juice to the cheese mixture, then beat until it is smooth. Mix in the chopped orange.

5 Dust a sheet of waxed paper thickly with confectioners' sugar. Carefully turn the roulade out onto the paper, then peel off the lining paper. Spread the filling over the roulade and roll up like a jelly roll. Transfer to a plate and dust with some more confectioners' sugar.

Chocolate, Date and Walnut Pudding

Puddings are not totally taboo when you're cutting calories or fat—this one stays
within the rules! Serve hot, with yogurt or skim-milk custard.

Serves 4

1 ounce (4 tablespoons)
chopped walnuts
1 ounce (2 tablespoons) chopped dates
2 eggs
1 teaspoon vanilla extract
2 tablespoons raw sugar
3 tablespoons whole-wheat flour
1 tablespoon cocoa powder
2 tablespoons skim milk

NUTRITION NOTES

Per portion
Calories	169
Fat	8.1g
Saturated Fat	1.7g
Cholesterol	96mg
Fiber	1.8g

1 Preheat the oven to 350°F. Grease
a 5-cup pudding bowl and place a
small circle of waxed paper or baking
parchment in the bottom. Spoon in the
walnuts and dates.

2 Separate the eggs and place the
yolks in a bowl with the vanilla and
sugar. Place the bowl over a pan of hot
water and beat until the mixture is thick
and pale.

3 Sift the flour and cocoa into the
mixture and fold them in with a metal
spoon. Stir in the milk to soften the
mixture slightly. Beat the egg whites
until they hold soft peaks and fold
them in.

4 Spoon the batter into the bowl and
bake for 40–45 minutes, or until the
pudding is well risen and firm to the
touch. Run a knife around the pudding to
loosen it from the bowl, and then turn it
out and serve right away.

Meringues

This is a basic meringue recipe. These light and airy mouthfuls are excellent served with low-fat whipped "cream."

1 Preheat the oven to 225°F. Grease and flour two large baking sheets.

2 With an electric mixer, beat the egg whites and salt in a very clean metal bowl on low speed. When they start to form soft peaks, add half the sugar and continue beating until the mixture holds stiff peaks.

3 With a large metal spoon, fold in the remaining sugar and vanilla or almond extract, if using.

4 Pipe the meringue mixture or gently spoon it onto the prepared sheets.

5 Bake for 2 hours. Turn off the oven. Loosen the meringues, invert, and set in another place on the sheets to prevent sticking. Leave in the oven as it cools. Serve sandwiched with low-fat whipped "cream," if desired.

Makes 24

4 egg whites
⅛ teaspoon salt
1¼ cups sugar
½ tsp vanilla or almond extract (optional)
1 cup low-fat whipped "cream" (optional)

NUTRITION NOTES

Per portion	
Calories	43
Fat	0
Saturated Fat	0
Cholesterol	0
Fiber	0

Snowballs

A variation on the basic meringue recipe, these snowballs are made with cornstarch.
They make an excellent accompaniment to ice cream.

Makes about 20

2 egg whites
½ cup sugar
1 tablespoon cornstarch, sifted
1 teaspoon white wine vinegar
¼ teaspoon vanilla extract

NUTRITION NOTES

Per portion	
Calories	29
Fat	0.01
Saturated Fat	0
Cholesterol	0
Fiber	0

1 Preheat the oven to 300°F. Line two baking sheets with baking parchment. Beat the egg whites in a large grease-free bowl until very stiff, using an electric mixer.

2 Add the sugar, beating until the meringue is very stiff. Beat in the cornstarch, vinegar and vanilla extract.

3 Drop teaspoonfuls of the mixture onto the baking sheets, shaping them into mounds, and bake for 30 minutes, until crisp.

4 Remove from the oven and allow to cool on the baking sheets. When the snowballs are cold, remove them from the baking paper with a spatula.

Brown Sugar Meringues

These light brown meringues are extremely low in fat and are delicious served on their own or sandwiched together with a fresh-fruit soft-cheese filling.

1 Preheat the oven to 325°F. Line two baking sheets with baking parchment. Press the sugar through a metal sieve into a bowl.

4 Sprinkle the meringues with the chopped walnuts. Bake for 30 minutes. Cool for 5 minutes on the baking sheets, then cool on a wire rack.

Makes about 20
¾ cup light brown sugar
2 egg whites
1 teaspoon finely chopped walnuts

NUTRITION NOTES
Per portion

Calories	197
Fat	6.8g
Saturated Fat	1.4g
Cholesterol	25mg
Fiber	0.7g

2 Beat the egg whites in a clean, dry bowl, until very stiff and dry, then beat in the sugar, about 1 tablespoon at a time until the meringue is very thick and glossy.

3 Spoon small mounds of the mixture onto the prepared baking sheets.

Raspberry Vacherin

Meringue rounds filled with orange-flavored fromage frais and fresh raspberries make a perfect dinner party dessert.

Serves 6
3 egg whites
¾ cup granulated sugar
1 teaspoon chopped almonds
confectioners' sugar, for dusting
raspberry leaves, to
decorate (optional)

For the filling
6 ounces (¾ cup) low-fat soft cheese
1–2 tablespoons honey
1 tablespoon Cointreau
½ cup low-fat fromage frais
8 ounces (1¼ cups) raspberries

Cook's Tip
When making the meringue, beat the egg whites until they are so stiff that you can turn the bowl upside down without them falling out.

NUTRITION NOTES
Per portion
Calories	248
Fat	2.22g
Saturated Fat	0.82g
Cholesterol	4mg
Fiber	1.06g

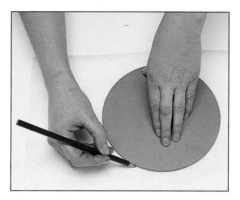

1 Preheat the oven to 275°F. Draw an 8-inch circle on two pieces of baking parchment. Turn the paper over so the marking is on the underside and use it to line two heavy baking sheets.

4 Bake for 1½–2 hours, then carefully lift the meringue rounds off the baking sheets, peel away the paper and cool on a wire rack.

2 Beat the egg whites in a grease-free bowl until very stiff, then gradually beat in the granulated sugar to make a stiff meringue mixture.

5 To make the filling, cream the soft cheese with the honey and liqueur in a bowl. Fold in the fromage frais and raspberries, reserving three of the best for decoration.

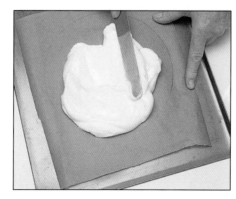

3 Spoon the mixture onto the circles on the prepared baking sheets, spreading the meringue evenly to·the edges. Sprinkle one meringue round with the chopped almonds.

6 Place the plain meringue round on a board, spread with the filling and top with the nut-covered round. Dust with confectioners' sugar, transfer to a serving plate and decorate with the reserved raspberries and a sprig of raspberry leaves, if desired.

Toasted Oat Meringues

The oats add an unusual flavor and texture to this interesting dessert.

Makes 12

¾ cup rolled oats

2 egg whites

⅛ teaspoon salt

1½ teaspoons cornstarch

¾ cup granulated sugar

NUTRITION NOTES

Per portion

Calories	98
Fat	0.8g
Saturated Fat	0.2g
Cholesterol	0
Fiber	0.6g

1 Preheat the oven to 275°F. Spread the oats on a baking sheet and toast in the oven until golden, about 10 minutes. Remove the oats and lower the heat to 250°F. Grease and flour a baking sheet.

Variation
Add ½ teaspoon ground cinnamon with the oats and fold in gently.

2 With an electric mixer, beat the egg whites and salt until they start to form soft peaks.

3 Sift over the cornstarch and continue beating until the whites hold stiff peaks. Add half the sugar and beat until glossy.

4 Add the remaining sugar and fold in, then fold in the toasted oats.

5 Gently spoon mounds of the mixture onto the prepared sheet and bake for 2 hours.

6 When done, turn off the oven. Lift the meringues from the baking sheet, turn over, and set in another place on the sheet to prevent sticking. Leave in the oven as it cools down.

Featherlight Peach Pudding

On chilly days, try this hot fruit pudding with its tantalizing sponge topping.

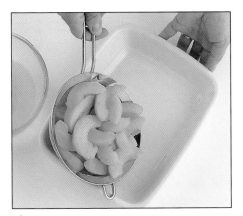

1 Preheat the oven to 350°F. Drain the peaches and place in a 4-cup pie dish with 2 tablespoons of the juice.

2 Put all the remaining ingredients, except the confectioners' sugar, into a mixing bowl. Beat for 3–4 minutes, until thoroughly combined.

3 Spoon the sponge mixture over the peaches and level the top evenly. Bake for 35–40 minutes, or until springy to the touch.

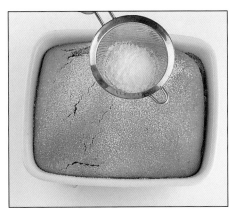

4 Lightly dust the top with confectioners' sugar before serving hot with the custard.

Cook's Tip

For a simple sauce, blend 1 teaspoon arrowroot with 1 tablespoon peach juice in a small saucepan. Stir in the remaining peach juice from the can and bring to a boil. Simmer for 1 minute, until thickened and clear.

Serves 4

14 ounces (3 cups) canned peach slices in natural juice
4 tablespoons low-fat spread
¼ cup light brown sugar
1 egg, beaten
½ cup whole-wheat flour
½ cup all-purpose flour
1 teaspoon baking powder
½ teaspoon ground cinnamon
¼ cup skim milk
½ teaspoon vanilla extract
2 teaspoons confectioners' sugar, for dusting
low-fat ready-to-serve custard, to serve

NUTRITION NOTES

Per portion

Calories	255
Fat	6.78g
Saturated Fat	1.57g
Cholesterol	35mg
Fiber	2.65g

Strawberry Torte

It's hard to believe that this delicious dessert is low in fat, but it's true, so enjoy!

Serves 6
2 eggs
⅓ cup granulated sugar
grated rind of ½ orange
½ cup all-purpose flour
strawberry leaves, to
decorate (optional)
confectioners' sugar, for dusting

For the filling
10 ounces (1¼ cups) low-fat soft
cheese
grated rind of ½ orange
2 tablespoons granulated sugar
4 tablespoons low-fat fromage frais
8 ounces strawberries, halved
¼ cup chopped
almonds, toasted

Cook's Tip
Use other soft fruits in season,
such as currants, raspberries,
blackberries or blueberries, or
try a mixture of different berries.

NUTRITION NOTES
Per portion

Calories	213
Fat	6.08g
Saturated Fat	1.84g
Cholesterol	70.22mg
Fiber	1.02g

1 Preheat the oven to 375°F. Grease a 12 x 8-in jelly roll pan and line with baking parchment.

2 In a bowl, beat the eggs, sugar and orange rind together with a handheld electric mixer until thick and mousselike (when the beaters are lifted, a trail should remain on the surface of the mixture for at least 15 seconds).

3 Fold in the flour with a metal spoon, being careful not to deflate. Turn into the prepared pan. Bake for 15–20 minutes, or until the cake springs back when lightly pressed. Turn the cake out onto a wire rack, remove the lining paper and let cool.

4 Meanwhile make the filling. In a bowl, mix the cheese with the orange rind, sugar and fromage frais until smooth. Divide between two bowls. Chop half the strawberry halves and add to one bowl of filling.

5 Cut the sponge widthwise into three equal pieces and sandwich them together with the strawberry filling. Spread two-thirds of the plain filling over the sides of the cake and press on the toasted almonds.

6 Spread the rest of the filling over the top of the cake and decorate with strawberry halves, and strawberry leaves if desired. Dust with confectioners' sugar and transfer to a serving plate.

Baked Blackberry Cheesecake

This light, low-fat cheesecake is best made with wild blackberries, if they're available, but cultivated ones will do; or substitute other soft fruit, such as loganberries, raspberries or blueberries.

Serves 5

6 ounces (¾ cup) low-fat cottage cheese
⅔ cup low-fat plain yogurt
1 tablespoon whole-wheat flour
2 tablespoons raw sugar
1 egg
1 egg white
finely grated rind and juice of ½ lemon
7 ounces (2 cups) fresh or frozen and thawed blackberries

Cook's Tip

If you prefer to use canned blackberries, choose those in natural juice and drain the fruit well before adding it to the cheesecake mixture. The juice can be served with the cheese-cake, but this will increase the total calories.

NUTRITION NOTES

Per portion
Calories	103
Fat	2g
Saturated Fat	0.8g
Cholesterol	41mg
Fiber	1.6g

1 Preheat the oven to 350°. Lightly grease and line a 7-inch layer-cake pan.

2 Place the cottage cheese in a food processor and process until smooth. Alternatively, rub it though a sieve to obtain a smooth mixture.

3 Add the yogurt, flour, sugar, egg and egg white, and mix. Add the lemon rind, juice and blackberries, reserving a few for decoration.

4 Pour the mixture into the prepared pan and bake it for 30–35 minutes, or until it is just set. Turn off the oven and leave for another 30 minutes.

5 Run a knife around the edge of the cheesecake and then turn it out. Remove the lining paper and place the cheesecake on a warm serving plate.

6 Decorate the cheesecake with the reserved blackberries and serve it warm.

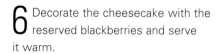

Cherry Clafoutis

When sweet cherries are in season, this makes a deliciously simple dessert for any occasion.
Serve warm with a little fromage frais.

Serves 6

3 cups fresh sweet cherries
½ cup all-purpose flour
pinch of salt
4 eggs, plus 2 egg yolks
½ cup sugar
2½ cups milk
4 tablespoons melted butter
sugar, for dusting

NUTRITION NOTES

Per portion

Calories	312
Fat	12.6g
Saturated Fat	2.9g
Cholesterol	198mg
Fiber	1g

1 Preheat the oven to 375°F. Lightly butter the bottom and sides of a shallow ovenproof dish. Pit the cherries and place in the dish.

2 Sift the flour and salt into a bowl. Add the eggs, egg yolks, sugar and a little of the milk and beat to a smooth batter.

3 Gradually beat in the rest of the milk and the butter, then strain the batter over the cherries. Bake for 40–50 minutes, until golden and just set. Serve warm, dusted with sugar, if you like.

Cook's Tip

Use two 15-ounce cans pitted black cherries, thoroughly drained, if fresh cherries are not available. For a special dessert, add 3 tablespoons kirsch to the batter.

Filo Fruit Baskets

These little baskets are an easy dinner party dessert.

1 Preheat the oven to 350°F. Grease six cups of a muffin pan.

2 Stack the filo sheets and cut with a sharp knife or scissors into 4½-inch squares.

3 Lay four squares of pastry in each of the six muffin cups. Press the pastry firmly into the cups, rotating slightly to make star-shaped baskets.

4 Brush the pastry baskets lightly with butter or margarine. Bake for 5–7 minutes, or until the pastry is crisp and golden. Cool on a wire rack.

5 In a bowl, lightly whip the cream until soft peaks form. Gently fold the strawberry preserves and orange liqueur into the cream.

6 Just before serving, spoon a little of the cream mixture into each pastry basket. Top with the fruit. Sprinkle with confectioners' sugar and decorate each basket with a small sprig of mint.

Serves 6

4 large or 8 small sheets filo pastry, thawed if frozen
5 tablespoons butter or margarine, melted
1 cup whipping cream
¼ cup strawberry preserves
1 tablespoon Cointreau or other orange liqueur
6 ounces (1 cup) seedless red grapes, halved
6 ounces (1 cup) seedless green grapes, halved
6 ounces (1 cup) fresh pineapple cubes
6 ounces (1 cup) raspberries
2 tablespoons confectioners' sugar
6 small sprigs of fresh mint, for garnishing

NUTRITION NOTES
Per portion

Calories	255
Fat	11g
Saturated Fat	2.2g
Cholesterol	1mg
Fiber	0.9g

Blueberry and Orange Crêpe Baskets

Impress your guests with these pretty, fruit-filled crêpes. When blueberries are not in season, replace them with other soft fruit, such as raspberries.

Serves 6
For the crêpes
1¼ cups all-purpose flour
pinch of salt
2 egg whites
1 cup skim milk
⅔ cup orange juice

For the filling
4 medium-size oranges
2 cups blueberries

Cook's Tip
Don't fill the pancake baskets until you're ready to serve them, because they will absorb the fruit juice and begin to soften.

NUTRITION NOTES
Per portion
Calories	159
Fat	0.5g
Saturated Fat	0.1g
Cholesterol	1mg
Fiber	3.3g

1 Preheat the oven to 400°F. To make the crêpes, sift the flour and salt into a bowl. Make a well in the center of the flour and add the egg whites, milk and orange juice. Beat hard, until all the liquid has been incorporated and the batter is smooth and bubbly.

2 Lightly grease a heavy or nonstick crêpe pan and heat until it is very hot. Pour in just enough batter to cover the base of the pan, swirling it to cover the pan evenly.

3 Cook until the crêpe has set and is golden, then turn it to cook the other side. Remove the crêpe to a sheet of absorbent paper towel, and then cook the remaining batter, to make 6–8 crêpes.

4 Place six small ovenproof bowls or molds on a baking sheet and arrange the crêpes over these. Bake the crêpes in the oven for about 10 minutes, until they are crisp and set into the shape of the molds. Carefully lift the "baskets" off the molds.

5 For the filling, pare a thin piece of orange rind from one orange and cut it in fine strips. Blanch the strips in boiling water for 30 seconds, rinse in cold water and set aside. Cut all the peel and white pith from all the oranges.

6 Divide the oranges into segments, catching the juice, combine with the blueberries and warm them gently. Spoon the fruit into the baskets and scatter the shreds of rind over the top. Serve with yogurt or light crème fraîche.

Filo and Apricot Purses

Filo pastry is very easy to use and is low in fat. Keep a box in the freezer ready for rustling up a speedy treat.

Makes 12
¾ cup dried apricots
3 tablespoons apricot compote
or conserve
3 amaretti cookies, crushed
3 sheets filo pastry
1 tablespoon plus 1 teaspoon soft
margarine, melted
confectioners' sugar, for dusting

NUTRITION NOTES

Per portion	
Calories	58
Fat	1.85g
Saturated Fat	0.4g
Cholesterol	0.12mg
Fiber	0.74g

1 Preheat the oven to 350°F. Grease two baking sheets. Chop the apricots, put them in a bowl and stir in the apricot compote. Add the crushed amaretti cookies and mix well.

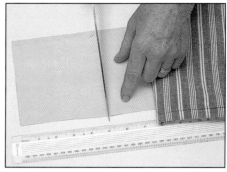

2 Cut the filo pastry into twenty-four 5-inch squares, pile the squares on top of each other and cover with a clean dish towel to prevent the pastry from drying out and becoming brittle.

3 Lay one pastry square on a flat surface, brush lightly with melted margarine, and lay another square diagonally on top. Brush the top square with melted margarine. Spoon a small mound of apricot mixture in the center of the pastry, bring up the edges and pinch together in a money-bag shape. Repeat with the remaining filo squares and filling to make 12 purses in all.

4 Arrange the purses on the prepared baking sheets and bake for 5–8 minutes, until golden brown. Transfer to a wire rack and dust lightly with confectioners' sugar. Serve warm.

Filo Scrunchies

Quick and easy to make, these pastries are ideal to serve as an afternoon snack. Eat them warm
or they will lose their crispness.

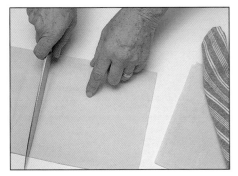

1 Preheat the oven to 375°F. Halve the
apricots or plums, remove the pits and
slice the fruit. Cut the filo pastry into
twelve 7-inch squares. Pile the squares
on top of each other and cover with a
clean dish towel to prevent the pastry
from drying out.

4 Place the scrunchies on a baking
sheet. Bake for 8–10 minutes, until
golden brown, then loosen the
scrunchies from the baking sheet with
a metal spatula and transfer to a wire
rack. Dust with confectioners' sugar and
serve at once.

Makes 6
5 apricots or plums
4 sheets filo pastry
4 teaspoons soft margarine, melted
⅓ cup raw sugar
2 tablespoons sliced almonds
confectioners' sugar, for dusting

NUTRITION NOTES
Per portion

Calories	132
Fat	4.19g
Saturated Fat	0.63g
Cholesterol	0
Fiber	0.67g

2 Remove one square of filo and brush
it with melted margarine. Lay a
second filo square on top, then, using
your fingers, mold the pastry into folds.
Make five more scrunchies in the same
way, working quickly so that the pastry
does not dry out.

3 Arrange a few slices of fruit in the
folds of each scrunchie, then sprinkle
generously with the raw sugar and
the almonds.

Plum Filo Pockets

These attractive party parcels are high in fiber as well as being a tasty treat.

Serves 4

4 ounces (½ cup) non-fat
milk soft cheese
1 tablespoon light brown sugar
½ teaspoon ground cloves
8 large, firm plums, halved and pitted
8 sheets filo pastry
sunflower oil, for brushing
confectioners' sugar, for sprinkling

NUTRITION NOTES

Per portion

Calories	188
Fat	1.87g
Saturated Fat	0.27g
Cholesterol	0.29mg
Fiber	2.55g

1 Preheat the oven to 425°F. Mix together the cheese, sugar and cloves.

2 Sandwich the plum halves back together with a spoonful of the cheese mixture in each plum.

3 Spread out the pastry and cut into 16 pieces, about 9 inches square. Brush one lightly with oil and place a second at a diagonal on top. Repeat with the remaining squares.

4 Place a plum on each pastry square and gather the corners together. Place on a baking sheet. Bake for 15–18 minutes, until golden, then dust with confectioners' sugar.

Apple Couscous Pudding

This unusual mixture makes a delicious family dessert with a rich, fruity flavor, but virtually no fat.

1 Preheat the oven to 400°F. Place the apple juice, couscous, golden raisins and spice in a pan and bring to a boil, stirring. Cover and simmer for 10–12 minutes, until all the liquid is absorbed.

3 Arrange the remaining apple slices overlapping on top and sprinkle with raw sugar. Bake for 25–30 minutes, or until golden brown. Serve hot, with low-fat yogurt.

Serves 4

2½ cups apple juice
4 ounces (⅔ cup) couscous
¼ cup golden rasins
½ teaspoon apple pie spice
1 large tart cooking apple, peeled, cored and sliced
2 tablespoons raw sugar
plain low-fat yogurt, to serve

NUTRITION NOTES

Per portion

Calories	194
Fat	0.58g
Saturated Fat	0.09g
Cholesterol	0
Fiber	0.75g

2 Spoon half the couscous mixture into a 5-cup ovenproof dish and top with half the apple slices. Top with the remaining couscous.

Filo Chiffon Pie

Filo pastry is low in fat and very easy to use. Here is an interesting and delicious alternative to more traditional rhubarb crumbles and pies.

Serves 3

1¼ pounds pink rhubarb
1 teaspoon apple pie spice
grated rind and juice of 1 orange
1 teaspoon granulated sweetener
1 tablespoon butter
3 sheets filo pastry

1 Preheat the oven to 400°F. Trim the leaves and ends from the rhubarb sticks and chop them into 1-inch pieces. Place them in a bowl.

3 Melt the butter and brush it over the pastry. Lift the pastry onto the pie dish, butter side up, and crumple it up to form a chiffon effect, covering the pie completely.

2 Add the apple pie spice, orange rind and juice and sweetener and toss well to coat evenly. Pour the rhubarb into a 4-cup pie dish.

4 Place the dish on a baking sheet and bake it for 20 minutes, until golden brown. Reduce the heat to 350°F and bake for another 10–15 minutes, until the rhubarb is tender. Serve warm.

Cook's Tip
Other fruit, such as apples, pears or peaches, can be used in this pie—try it with whatever is in season.

NUTRITION NOTES
Per portion

Calories	158
Fat	5.3g
Saturated Fat	1g
Cholesterol	0.4mg
Fiber	2.4g

Mango and Amaretti Strudel

Fresh mango and crushed amaretti cookies wrapped in wafer-thin filo pastry make a special treat that is equally delicious made with apricots or plums.

Serves 4

1 large mango
grated rind of 1 lemon
2 amaretti cookies
3 tablespoons raw sugar
4 tablespoons whole-wheat
bread crumbs
2 sheets filo pastry, each
18 x 11 inches
4 teaspoons soft margarine, melted
1 tablespoon chopped almonds
confectioners' sugar, for dusting

Cook's Tip

The easiest way to prepare a mango is to cut horizontally through the fruit, keeping the knife blade close to the pit. Repeat on the other side of the pit and peel off the skin. Remove the remaining skin and flesh from around the pit.

NUTRITION NOTES

Per portion

Calories	239
Fat	8.45g
Saturated Fat	4.43g
Cholesterol	17.25mg
Fiber	3.3g

1 Preheat the oven to 375°F. Lightly grease a large baking sheet. Halve, pit and peel the mango. Cut the flesh into cubes, then place them in a bowl and sprinkle with grated lemon rind.

2 Crush the amaretti cookies and mix them with the raw sugar and the whole-wheat bread crumbs.

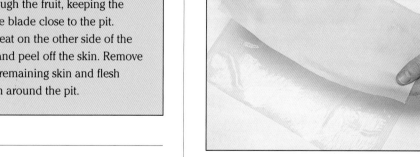

3 Lay one sheet of filo on a flat surface and brush with a quarter of the melted margarine. Top with the second sheet, brush with one-third of the remaining margarine, then fold both sheets over, if necessary, to make a rectangle measuring 11 x 9 inches. Brush with half the remaining margarine.

4 Sprinkle the filo with the amaretti mixture, leaving a 2-inch border on each long side. Arrange the mango cubes over the top.

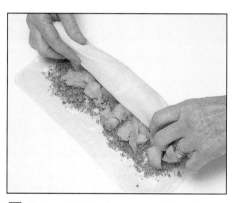

5 Roll up the filo from one of the long sides, jelly roll-style. Lift the strudel onto the baking sheet with the seam underneath. Brush with the remaining melted margarine and sprinkle with the chopped almonds.

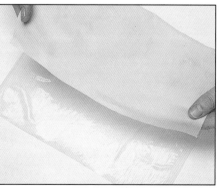

6 Bake for 20–25 minutes, until golden brown, then transfer to a board. Dust with the confectioners' sugar, slice diagonally and serve warm.

Chunky Apple Bread Pudding

This filling, economical family dessert is a good way to use up slightly stale bread—any type of bread will do, but whole-wheat is richest in fiber.

Serves 4

1 pound tart cooking apples
3 ounces whole-wheat bread, without crusts
½ cup low-fat cottage cheese
3 tablespoons light brown sugar
1 cup low-fat milk
1 teaspoon raw sugar

Cook's Tip

You may need to adjust the amount of milk used, depending on the dryness of the bread; the more stale the bread, the more milk it will absorb.

NUTRITION NOTES

Per portion

Calories	168
Fat	1g
Saturated Fat	0.4g
Cholesterol	2mg
Fiber	2.9g

1 Preheat the oven to 425°F. Peel the apples, cut them into quarters and remove the cores.

2 Roughly chop the apples into even-size pieces, about ½ inch across.

3 Cut the bread into ½-inch dice.

4 Toss together the apples, bread, cottage cheese and brown sugar in a bowl.

5 Stir in the milk and then pour the mixture into a wide ovenproof dish. Sprinkle with the raw sugar.

6 Bake for 30–35 minutes, or until golden brown and bubbling. Serve hot.

Baked Apples in Honey and Lemon

A classic mix of flavors in a healthy, traditional family pudding. Serve warm, with skim-milk custard.

Serves 4
4 medium-size cooking apples
1 tablespoon honey
grated rind and juice of 1 lemon
1 tablespoon low-fat spread

NUTRITION NOTES
Per portion

Calories	65
Fat	1.7g
Saturated Fat	0.4g
Cholesterol	0
Fiber	1.7g

1 Preheat the oven to 350°F. Remove the cores from the apples, leaving them whole.

2 With a zester or sharp knife, cut lines though the apple skin at intervals and place in an ovenproof dish.

3 Mix together the honey, lemon rind, juice and low-fat spread.

4 Spoon the mixture into the apples and cover the dish with foil or a lid. Bake for 40–45 minutes, or until the apples are tender. Serve with skim-milk custard.

Strawberry and Apple Crumble

A high fibere, healthier version of the classic apple crumble. Raspberries can be used instead of strawberries, either fresh or frozen. Serve warm, with skim-milk custard.

1 Preheat the oven to 350°F. Peel, core and slice the apples. Halve the strawberries.

2 Toss together the apples, strawberries, sweetener, cinnamon and orange juice. Pour into a 5-cup ovenproof dish or four individual dishes.

3 Combine the flour and oats in a bowl and mix in the low-fat spread with a fork.

4 Sprinkle the crumble evenly over the fruit. Bake for 40–45 minutes (20–25 minutes for individual dishes), until golden brown and bubbling. Serve warm, with low-fat custard or yogurt.

Serves 4

1 pound cooking apples
5 ounces (1¼ cups) strawberries, hulled
2 tablespoons granulated sweetener
½ teaspoon ground cinnamon
2 tablespoons orange juice

For the crumble

3 tablespoons whole-wheat flour
⅔ cup rolled oats
2 tablespoons low-fat spread

NUTRITION NOTES

Per portion

Calories	182
Fat	4g
Saturated Fat	0.9g
Cholesterol	0
Fiber	3.5g

Mixed Berry Tart

The orange-flavored pastry of this tart is delicious with the fresh fruits of summer.
Serve this with some extra shreds of orange rind scattered on top.

Serves 8
For the pastry
2 cups all-purpose flour
8 tablespoons (1 stick) unsalted butter
finely grated rind of 1 orange, plus
extra to decorate

For the filling
1¼ cups crème fraîche
finely grated rind of 1 lemon
2 teaspoons confectioners' sugar
1½ pounds (6 cups) mixed
summer berries

1 To make the pastry, put the flour and butter in a large bowl. Rub in the butter until the mixture resembles bread crumbs.

2 Add the orange rind and enough cold water to make a soft dough.

3 Roll into a ball and chill for at least 20 minutes. Roll out the pastry on a lightly floured surface.

4 Line a 9-inch loose-bottomed tart pan with the pastry. Chill for 30 minutes. Preheat the oven to 400°F and place a baking sheet in the oven to heat up. Weight the pastry shell with waxed paper and baking beans and bake blind on the baking sheet for 15 minutes. Remove the paper and beans and bake the pastry for 10 minutes, until golden. Allow to cool.

5 To make the filling, beat the crème fraîche, lemon rind and sugar together and pour into the pastry shell. Top with fruit, sprinkle with orange rind and serve sliced.

NUTRITION NOTES
Per portion
Calories	293
Fat	17.9g
Saturated Fat	5.9g
Cholesterol	40mg
Fiber	2.4g

Crunchy Gooseberry Crumble

Gooseberries are perfect for traditional family desserts like this one. If you can't find them, other fruits such as apples, plums or rhubarb can be used instead.

Serves 4

1¼ pounds (5 cups) gooseberries
4 tablespoons granulated sugar
1 cup rolled oats
¾ cup whole-wheat flour
4 tablespoons sunflower oil
4 tablespoons raw sugar
2 tablespoons chopped walnuts
low-fat yogurt or custard, to serve

NUTRITION NOTES

Per portion

Calories	422
Fat	18.5g
Saturated Fat	2.32g
Cholesterol	0
Fiber	5.12g

1 Preheat the oven to 400°F. Place the gooseberries in a pan with the granulated sugar. Cover the pan and cook over a low heat for 10 minutes, until the gooseberries are just tender. Pour into an ovenproof dish.

2 To make the crumble, place the oats, flour and oil in a bowl, and stir with a fork until evenly mixed.

3 Stir in the raw sugar and walnuts, then spread evenly over the gooseberries. Bake for 25–30 minutes, or until golden and bubbling. Serve hot with low-fat yogurt, or custard made with skim milk.

Cook's Tip

The best cooking gooseberries are the early small, firm green ones.

Ginger Upside-Down Cake

A traditional dessert goes down well on a cold winter day. This one is quite quick to make and looks very impressive.

1 Preheat the oven to 350°F. For the topping, brush the bottom and sides of a 9-inch round springform cake pan with oil. Sprinkle the brown sugar over the bottom.

2 Arrange the peaches cut side down in the pan with a walnut half in each.

3 Sift together the flour, baking soda, ginger and cinnamon, then stir in the sugar. Beat together the egg, milk and oil, then mix into the dry ingredients until smooth.

4 Pour the mixture evenly over the peaches and bake for 35–40 minutes, until firm to the touch. Turn out onto a serving plate. Serve hot with low-fat yogurt or custard.

Serves 4–6
sunflower oil, for brushing
1 tablespoon brown sugar
4 medium peaches, halved and pitted, or 8 canned peach halves
8 walnut halves

For the base
½ cup whole-wheat flour
½ teaspoon baking soda
1½ teaspoons ground ginger
1 teaspoon ground cinnamon
½ cup dark brown sugar
1 egg
½ cup skim milk
¼ cup sunflower oil

NUTRITION NOTES
Per portion
Calories	432
Fat	16.54g
Saturated Fat	2.27g
Cholesterol	48.72mg
Fiber	4.79g

Latticed Peaches

An elegant dessert; it certainly doesn't look low in fat, but it really is. Use canned peach halves when fresh peaches are out of season, or if you're short of time.

Serves 6
For the pastry
1 cup all-purpose flour
3 tablespoons butter or
sunflower margarine
3 tablespoons low-fat plain yogurt
2 tablespoons orange juice
skim milk, for glaze

For the filling
3 ripe peaches or nectarines
3 tablespoons ground almonds
2 tablespoons low-fat plain yogurt
finely grated rind of 1 small orange
¼ teaspoon almond extract

For the sauce
1 ripe peach or nectarine
3 tablespoons orange juice

Cook's Tip
This dessert is best eaten fairly fresh from the oven, as the pastry can toughen slightly if left to stand. Assemble the peaches in their pastry on a baking sheet, chill in the refrigerator, and bake just before serving.

NUTRITION NOTES
Per portion
Calories	219
Fat	10.8g
Saturated Fat	1.6g
Cholesterol	1mg
Fiber	2.4g

1 For the pastry, sift the flour into a bowl and, using your fingertips, rub in the butter or margarine evenly. Stir in the yogurt and orange juice to bind the mixture into a firm dough.

2 Roll out about half the pastry thinly and use a pastry cutter to stamp out rounds about 3 inches in diameter, slightly larger than the circumference of the peaches. Place on a lightly greased baking sheet.

3 Peel the peaches or nectarines, halve and remove the pits. Mix together the almonds, yogurt, orange rind and almond extract. Spoon into the hollows of each peach half and place, cut side down, on the pastry rounds.

4 Roll out the remaining pastry thinly and cut into thin strips. Arrange the strips over the peaches to form a lattice, brushing with milk to secure firmly. Trim off the ends neatly.

5 Chill in the refrigerator for 30 minutes. Preheat the oven to 400°F. Brush with milk and bake for 15–18 minutes, until golden brown.

6 For the sauce, peel the peach or nectarine and halve it to remove the pit. Place the flesh in a food processor with the orange juice, and purée it until smooth. Serve the peaches hot, with the peach sauce spooned around.

Hot Plum Pandowdy

Other fruits can be used in place of plums, depending on the season. Canned cherries are also a convenient pantry substitute.

Serves 4

1 pound ripe red plums,
quartered and pitted
1 cup skim milk
4 tablespoons powdered non-fat milk
1 tablespoon light brown sugar
1 teaspoon vanilla extract
¾ cup self-rising flour
2 egg whites
confectioners' sugar, to sprinkle

NUTRITION NOTES

Per portion

Calories	195
Fat	0.48g
Saturated Fat	0.12g
Cholesterol	2.8mg
Fiber	2.27g

1 Preheat the oven to 425°F. Lightly oil a wide, shallow ovenproof dish and add the plums.

2 Pour the milk, powdered milk, sugar, vanilla, flour and egg whites into a food processor. Process until smooth.

3 Pour the batter over the plums. Bake for 25–30 minutes, or until well risen and golden. Sprinkle with confectioners' sugar and serve immediately.

Glazed Apricot Sponge

Puddings can be very high in saturated fat, but this one uses the minimum of oil and no eggs.

1 Preheat the oven to 350°F. Lightly oil a 3¾-cup pudding bowl. Spoon in the syrup.

3 Mix the flour, bread crumbs, sugar and cinnamon, then beat in the oil and milk. Spoon into the pudding bowl and bake for 50–55 minutes, or until firm and golden. Turn out and serve with the puréed fruit as a sauce.

Serves 4

2 teaspoons golden syrup or light corn syrup
14½-ounce can apricot halves in fruit juice
1¼ cups self-rising flour
1½ cups fresh bread crumbs
⅔ cup light brown sugar
1 teaspoon ground cinnamon
2 tablespoons sunflower oil
¾ cup skim milk

NUTRITION NOTES

Per portion

Calories	364
Fat	6.47g
Saturated Fat	0.89g
Cholesterol	0.88mg
Fiber	2.37g

2 Drain the apricots and reserve the juice. Arrange about 8 halves in the bowl. Purée the rest of the apricots with the juice and set aside.

Fruity Bread Pudding

A delicious family favorite dessert from grandmother's day, with a lighter, healthier touch.

Serves 4

⅔ cup mixed dried fruit
⅔ cup apple juice
2 cups diced stale whole-wheat or
white bread
1 teaspoon apple pie spice
1 large banana, sliced
⅔ cup skim milk
1 tablespoon raw sugar
plain low-fat yogurt, to serve

NUTRITION NOTES

Per portion
Calories	190
Fat	0.89g
Saturated Fat	0.21g
Cholesterol	0.75mg
Fiber	1.8g

1 Preheat the oven to 400°F. Place the dried fruit in a small pan with the apple juice and bring to a boil.

2 Remove the pan from the heat and stir in the bread, spice and banana. Spoon the mixture into a shallow 5-cup ovenproof dish and pour the milk on top.

3 Sprinkle with raw sugar and bake for 25–30 minutes, until firm and golden brown. Serve hot or cold with plain low-fat yogurt.

Cook's Tip
Different types of bread will absorb varying amounts of liquid, so you may need to adjust the amount of milk to allow for this.

Souffléed Orange Semolina Pudding

Semolina pudding has a reputation as a rather dull dessert, but cooked like this you would hardly recognize it.

1 Preheat the oven to 400°F. Place the semolina in a nonstick pan with the milk and sugar. Stir over moderate heat until thickened and smooth. Remove from the heat.

3 Beat the egg white until stiff but not dry, then fold lightly and evenly into the mixture. Spoon into a 4-cup oven-proof dish and bake for 15–20 minutes, until risen and golden brown. Serve immediately.

2 Grate a few long shreds of orange rind from the orange and save for decoration. Finely grate the remaining rind. Cut all the peel and white pith from the orange and remove the segments. Stir the fruit into the semolina with the orange rind.

Serves 4

¼ cup semolina
2½ cups low-fat milk
2 tablespoons light brown sugar
1 large orange
1 egg white

NUTRITION NOTES

Per portion

Calories	158
Fat	2.67g
Saturated Fat	1.54g
Cholesterol	10.5mg
Fiber	0.86g

Cook's Tip

When using the rind of citrus fruit, scrub the fruit thoroughly before use, or buy unwaxed fruit.

Souffléed Rice Pudding

The fluffy egg whites in this unusually light rice pudding make the portions seem much more substantial, without adding lots of extra calories or fat.

Serves 4

¼ cup short-grain rice
3 tablespoons honey
3¾ cups low-fat milk
1 vanilla bean or ½ teaspoon
vanilla extract
2 egg whites
1 teaspoon freshly grated nutmeg

Cook's Tip

If you wish, use skim milk
instead of low-fat, but take care
when it's simmering, because it
tends to boil over very easily.

NUTRITION NOTES

Per portion

Calories	161
Fat	0.9g
Saturated Fat	0.1g
Cholesterol	4mg
Fiber	0

1 Place the rice, honey and milk in a heavy or nonstick pan and bring the milk to a boil. Add the vanilla bean, if using it.

2 Reduce the heat and put the lid on the pan. Let simmer gently for 1–1¼ hours, stirring occasionally to prevent sticking, until most of the liquid has been absorbed.

3 Remove the vanilla bean, or if using vanilla extract, add this to the rice mixture now. Preheat the oven to 425°F.

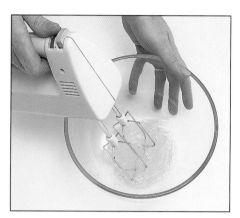

4 Place the egg whites in a clean, dry bowl and beat them until they hold soft peaks.

5 Using a metal spoon or spatula, fold the egg whites evenly into the rice mixture and tip into a 4-cup ovenproof dish.

6 Sprinkle with grated nutmeg and bake for 15–20 minutes, until the pudding is well risen and golden brown. Serve hot.

Index

Acknowledgments

The publishers would like to thank the following contributing authors: Catherine Atkinson, Jacqueline Clark, Frances Cleary, Anne Clevely, Roz Denny, Joanna Farrow, Christine France, Linda Fraser, Shirley Gill, Carole Handslip, Shezad Husain, Annie Nichols, Maggie Pannell, Katherine Richmond, Anne Sheasby, Liz Trigg and Laura Washburn.

    The publishers would like to thank the following photographers: Karl Adamson, Steve Baxter, James Duncan, Michelle Garrett, Amanda Heywood, Don Last and Michael Michaels.